Praise for
The Cowboy Call

"Dale Hirschman has always had a story to tell. In his vast well of relationships, he has remembered and shares here with us the stories of how our everyday lives are true experiences with God."

—Susie McEntire, Christian country performer,
Positive Country Music Artist of the Year

"Through my high school and college rodeo career I've enjoyed listening to many of Dale's church services and testimonies. Dale's ministries helped shape and nurture my own Christian walk. I hope God speaks to you through these real-life stories just like He did me."

—Trell Etbauer, PRCA cowboy
and three time Linderman Award winner

"Dale has done a great job of putting together and illustrating this collection of stories that are birthed from having a relationship with a loving Father through Jesus Christ."

—Corey Navarre, PBR and WNFR Finals qualifier

THE
COWBOY
CALL

THE
COWBOY
CALL
Living for Jesus in the Western World

written and illustrated by

Dale Hirschman

TATE PUBLISHING & *Enterprises*

Scripture quotations marked (NIV) are taken from the Holy Bible, New International Version®, NIV®. Copyright © 1973, 1978, 1984 by Biblica, Inc.™ Used by permission of Zondervan. All rights reserved worldwide. www.zondervan.com

Scripture quotations marked (NKJV) are taken from the New King James Version®. Copyright © 1982 by Thomas Nelson, Inc. Used by permission. All rights reserved.

Scripture quotations marked (KJV) are taken from the Holy Bible, King James Version, Cambridge, 1769. Used by permission. All rights reserved.

The opinions expressed by the author are not necessarily those of Tate Publishing, LLC.

Published by Tate Publishing & Enterprises, LLC
127 E. Trade Center Terrace | Mustang, Oklahoma 73064 USA
1.888.361.9473 | www.tatepublishing.com

Tate Publishing is committed to excellence in the publishing industry. The company reflects the philosophy established by the founders, based on Psalm 68:11,
"The Lord gave the word and great was the company of those who published it."

Book design copyright © 2010 by Tate Publishing, LLC. All rights reserved.
Cover design by Leah LeFlore
Interior design by Blake Brasor
Illustrations by Dale Hirschman

Published in the United States of America

ISBN: 978-1-61739-417-1
1. Religion / Christian Life / Devotional
2. Religion / Christian Life / Personal Growth
10.12.27

Dedication

I would like to dedicate this book to the men and women
who have taken the ultimate challenge of following Jesus
Christ daily, regardless of what path of life they might be
traveling, they have set their lives apart from this world
and are letting their lights shine. To those, I say thank you,
and I want you to know that you are my heroes.

Acknowledgments

I would like to thank my wife, Sarah, and my daughters, Rachel and Rebekah, for their support, love, and prayers as they encourage me to trust God for the best in life.

I would also like to thank Linda Thomas and Karen Hardin for all of their proofreading and encouragement to pursue this project until it became a reality.

My thanks go out to my friends who have been a part of an exciting life of following Jesus. And we ain't finished yet.

I am most grateful to my Lord and Savior, Jesus Christ, who died for my sins, who chose me and empowered me so that my life will make a positive difference in this world.

To my readers, a special thanks to you for reading this book. I want you to know that your life counts, and God has great plans for you.

Table of Contents

Foreword

I have known Dale Hirschman for nearly thirty years. His life has been a great example of genuine Christianity at work. From our college days years ago to today, Dale has been a true witness for the Lord wherever he has been. Dale competed in college rodeos and then in the professional ranks in the PRCA riding bareback horses. The rodeo atmosphere, especially in those days, was very anti-Christian, to say the least. Dale never wavered. He just kept being faithful and walking it out. So I wasn't surprised years back when I heard that he was in the ministry. For thirty years or so, he has been doing the ministry at all the college rodeos in the Central Plains region of Oklahoma and Kansas. His faithfulness in that realm has left a trail of young cowboys, cowgirls, and rodeo and non-rodeo people touched by the Lord Jesus Christ, and His grace. Dale's low-impact style of evangelism and his love for these college kids is an incredible witness to those of us observing from a distance. Our culture has witnessed the advent, in recent years, of the cowboy church movement. It is interesting to note that Dale was doing cowboy church when cowboy church wasn't cool.

You're going to love Dale's book. He's proven himself here to be a good storyteller. And to make it even better, the stories are all true. He has a knack for communicating his devotion to the Lord in a very practical way. These stories will make you laugh and cry. But I believe the real value in this book is the simple trusting of the Lord in everyday circumstances. You'll enjoy it, and your faith will be inspired, maybe even to the degree that you will be moved to start trusting the Lord in the daily affairs of your own life. Thanks, Dale, for making it real.

—Pastor Andy Taylor
Trinity Fellowship
Sayre, Oklahoma

DALE HIRSCHMAN

Preface

For decades, rodeo cowboys held the reputation of being beer-drinking, woman-chasing, barroom-brawling hoodlums—a reputation many cowboys went above and beyond to earn. However, in the early 1970s, some cowboys went about changing that image. Several cowboys who professed a relationship with Jesus Christ decided to step into the light with their Christian faith. The cowboys got together with Tom Landry, the head coach for the Dallas Cowboys, and began a Christian cowboy organization under the headship of the Fellowship of Christian Athletes.

The group of cowboys held a couple of small meetings and decided to hold a church service for other cowboys right at the rodeo arena. The attendance for the first church service was diminutive but promising. Plans were made for another church service at another rodeo, and attendance grew tremendously. The small group of cowboys was well on its way to ushering in a move of God into the rodeo and western world.

From these humble beginnings, several cowboys started breaking ground into the hard-core rodeo world. Glenn and Ann Smith, Coy and Donna Huffman, Russ and Randy Weaver, Dennis McKinley, Mark Schricker, Wilbur Plaugher, Ron Conaster, and Paul and Linda Schultz were some of the few who stepped up to the mountainous challenge. These men and women helped chip away and clear a path for other ministers to follow, people such as Ted and Linda Wiese, Ronnie Christian, myself, and many others.

Cowboy churches have sprung up in various forms across the country. The first cowboy churches were just like the ones mentioned earlier, services held at rodeos for the traveling cowboys. Other cowboy Bible studies and church services started being held regularly in one location, such as a rodeo arena right before a practice or a jackpot. Still others moved into or built a building and were recognized as a regular church geared toward the western world. Some cowboy churches have even occupied cattle sale barns on off nights during the week. Wherever they could, they would meet and share the Word of God.

Whether a traveling ministry, such as my family is involved in, or a ministry in a permanent location, the cowboy church has been a rapidly growing movement of God. One of the reasons for the success of these services is the fact that they definitely have a "come as you are" atmosphere, physically and emotionally. People tend to feel comfortable at the cowboy church services and can be themselves. One young lady told me after a college rodeo church service that that was the first time she had been to church because she didn't wear dresses. Cowboys will come straight from work, covered with mud and blood (and probably some of them covered with beer). We actually had one cowboy come to church while he was still drunk from the night before. A couple of his friends sat on each side of him as he swayed back and forth, listening to the fact that Jesus loved him. As he stumbled out after church, I sincerely thanked him for coming. He smiled and said thanks.

Another time, while I was teaching a Bible study in Sunday school, one individual became a little vocal, and some listeners took it as him being out of line. Afterward, there was a discussion between the younger cowboys in attendance as to whether or not they should "take the individual out back and beat the hell out of him." Now, is that the way God wants us to respond? No, but that's what those guys felt at the time. Does God want us to stay that way, to feel like we ought to whip someone when we don't agree with them? No, but if you ever attend one of my Sunday school classes, you might want to behave. Some cowboys in attendance tend to be a little rough around the edges, but they come and hear about the love of Jesus.

The aspect of ministry that my wife and I are involved in is the traveling part, as I mentioned earlier. We travel to various rodeos and hold church services for the cowboys and cowgirls. Our main focus is to the college rodeos in the Central Plains region, Oklahoma and Kansas. We also minister at junior rodeos, regional rodeos, and professional rodeos. I held my first cowboy church service in Durant, Oklahoma, while I was still a contestant in college rodeos. The year was 1980, and I've continued to hold cowboy church services ever since that time. In 1991, my wife and I were married; and three years later, our family started growing. Now she and our girls travel with me whenever possible.

We usually hold church right at the arena, so we deal with weather of all types. We've had church in the pouring rain, snow, high winds, dust, and heat. We've all stood in an announcer's stand for the entire church service while it was pouring rain outside. We've had church sitting around an old, pot-bellied stove during the winter time in an indoor arena; and we've baked under a hot sun with no breeze.

We've baptized people in old bathtubs, whirlpools, horse tanks, and lakes in all types of weather. Not counting dogs, we've had attendance that has ranged from four people to three hundred or more people. We've had people accept Jesus while they sat on their horses, waiting for their turn to compete. We've even had to dodge past a fighting bull that got loose right before church. I've been "baptized" by a water truck while it was watering the arena during a cowboy church service. Whether we've left church hot, cold, dusty, muddy, or wet, we've always left blessed.

DALE HIRSCHMAN

Introduction

Welcome. Throughout the years, I've been blessed to realize that God has specific plans for my life. I believe with all my heart those plans included me being a rodeo cowboy. During that time in my life, I dedicated myself to Jesus Christ and have tried to live for Him, even when it wasn't cool to be a Christian cowboy. Oftentimes, I was the only one who professed to be a Christian, and other times I had Christian brothers to rodeo with. The latter is by far the best, but it is important to walk the walk either way.

My rodeoing has had good times as well as bad times. I've been successful, and I've experienced failure more than I wanted to—some my fault; other times for reasons that I don't know. I know the feeling of making an exceptional ride, and I know the feeling of getting body-slammed so hard that you don't know the way back to the bucking chutes. I've experienced long droughts of not winning and the times where they write you a check almost everywhere you go. As God has called me into the rodeo ministry, I can relate to both those who have been successful as well as those who battle discouragement at almost every turn. Whether a person is on top of the world or on the bottom, quite often, they battle the same things.

Another portion of my life has been the love of being in God's creation, the great outdoors. As a young child I grew up spending time on my grandparents' farm. From the exploration of creeks and streams to the curiosity of what's over the next hill, an unquenchable thirst for the solitude and peace of being outdoors has engulfed me. I can relate to why Jesus went to the wilderness and not the shopping mall to pray!

Even though time has brought a close to me spending outings on my grandparents' farm, the thirst for the great outdoors has been revived in me through hunting. It was through rodeo that I met the people who introduced me to the great sport of hunting. And through hunting I have seen the fingerprint of God on my life again! Each year I submerge myself in the soul reviving beauty of God's creation. As I settle into a deer blind and become quiet, I am still, and I do know that He is God!

The following stories are testimonies of the faithfulness of God, both in the world of rodeo and the world of hunting. I have written them the very best that I remember. If I've missed any detail, it was purely an accident. I regretfully apologize for any names I unintentionally left out while writing the following stories. I hate it when I forget names, but I realize that I'm not the only one who does that.

The stories that follow are not to be deep, new, heavy teaching revelations from God. They are meant to encourage you to follow more closely after Jesus and hopefully give you the boost to take a bolder stand for Him. My life was saved by the preaching of the gospel of Jesus, but the testimonies of His faithfulness are what really got me to trust Him more. So I hope you enjoy the word pictures

DALE HIRSCHMAN

that I've tried to paint in your head as you read 'bout the faithfulness of Jesus Christ, our Lord.

As Unto the Lord

Whenever a student shows superior effort and abilities at several Lyle Sankey Rodeo Schools, Lyle often invites them to come back and help instruct at another school. Such was the case for a student who we'll, for practical purposes, call Dave. Dave had been a student at several of Lyle's schools and had risen above the norm in both his rodeo skills and his Christian walk. With Lyle's schools placing emphasis on the life of walking with Jesus as much as developing rodeo skills, Dave fit the mode extremely well.

Thanksgiving weekend, Lyle Sankey and Abbyville, Kansas, all converged to host the Thanksgiving rodeo school, where Dave would make his debut as an instructor. Lyle's desire is that a student gets what he pays for at his rodeo schools; thus, they are very organized, and there is seldom any down time. Rodeo is not like a Tiddleywinks tournament; students and sometimes instructors endure body slams, pulled muscles, and loss of blood and skin. A rodeo school is an endurance test, both mentally and physically, for all those involved. Armed with Colossians 3:23 (NIV), "Whatever you do, work at it with all your heart, as working for the Lord, and not for man," Dave was ready to step up to the plate and do his part.

Arrival at Abbyville early the first day found people swarming around like folks at the DVD bargain bin at Wal-Mart. Every member of the school, staff and student, hurried to find his or her place. The students desperately tried to look tough and confident instead of as lost as geese in a snowstorm. Even though announcements had been made, several wandered around, searching for their event's meeting area. Members finally sorted into their designated areas, and the students, with their spurs on the wrong feet or on upside down, started their nervous stories of how they'd been rodeoing for quite some time and were there just to tune up.

It was during one of these times that Dave approached Lyle to let him know he was available to help instruct.

Now, Dave might have talked to Lyle earlier. I just don't know if he did. However, the answer that Dave got was not at all what he expected.

"We've got all the instructors that we can handle with the number of students that we have. You might go to the arena and ask Bronc Rumford, the stock contractor, if he needs any help with the stock," responded Lyle. Dave's goal was to do "all things as unto the Lord, and not unto man"; so, somewhat disappointed with the response that he received, he headed to the arena. Every job is important at any type of function, whether it's mud-wrestling, hog-callin,' or a rodeo school. But when you have your heart set and you're pumped up to be an instructor, the air gets let out of your balloon when that falls through.

Arriving at the arena, Dave found the typical pre-rodeo activities: the sounds of horses running, snorting, and blowing; gates banging and clanging; and cowboys shouting to turn the overanxious broncs and bulls. The air was filled with dust and the aroma of hay, horses, and recycled grass. The pecking order was being established in the bull pens as the bovines fought to rise to the top of the hierarchy of "Bramers." Dave found Bronc Rumford in the midst of all the fun and excitement and inquired if he needed any help with loading and sorting the stock.

Bronc's response was, "Nope. Got all the help I need."

Dave dropped his sights to a lot less glamorous job than loading stock, still wanting to do all things "as unto the Lord."

"Do you need any help on the stripping chute?"

"Nope. We've got a couple of local boys to help there."

During the first few hours of the first day, Dave's morale was taking some tremendous blows. But his determination to do all things as unto the Lord would not waver as he asked Bronc one more time, "Is there anything that you need help with?"

"Yes, there is," Bronc replied as he gazed around the area. Sometimes there is that tone in a person's voice that makes you think, *Oh no. What's next?* And this was one of those times. Spying an old porcelain bathtub laying upside-down, Bronc proclaimed, "I need a place to water my horses. Take that old tub, clean it out, plug it up, and fill 'er up so I can water my horses. Thanks, pard."

Bronc walked off. Doing all things "as unto the Lord" just hit rock bottom as Dave trudged to the discarded bathtub.

Whenever you indulge in any activity in the cowboy world, there is a definite spirit of pride and individualism involved, which can be both good and bad. Heaving an old bathtub right-side-up in a ditch and then scrubbing it out involves a large degree of ego swallowing. Not knowing where the tub came from, whose it was, or what was in it didn't help matters any. After scraping and scrubbing all the foreign matter out of the old tub, Dave tackled the next problem of trying to plug the three-inch-wide drain hole. "As unto the Lord" was sure making Dave pay a price.

Searching for just the right size of object to shove in that hole had Dave looking in the back of pickups, under the bleachers, and anywhere else he could think to look. His search for the tub plug found him looking in a nearby tree. And the size and shape of the plug was there, about twelve feet up in the tree. All he needed to cut that branch was a saw, and he would be in business. Saws usually are not just lying around, especially at a rodeo arena; so back to the pickups he went to look for a saw in the bed of someone's pickup. A fruitless search left Dave with only one option, and that was to ask Bronc if he had one. Bronc informed him that he did not have a saw, but there was a hand ax behind the seat of his pickup. That would have to do.

Up into the tree Dave scurried to retrieve the perfect-sized plug for the tub. As Dave tore into the tree branch, he discovered that the ax was as sharp as a nail—the side of the nail, not the point. As he whacked and hacked at the tree, he kept repeating to himself,

"As ... unto ... the ... Lord. As ... unto ... the ... Lord." Finally, after close to an eternity, Dave freed that limb from the rest of the tree. Dragging the branch out of the tree and over to the tub, Dave whittled it down to the right size. After wrapping some inner tube around it, Dave took the old ax and gladly drove that stake into the heart of the drain hole. Stepping back to watch the tub as he filled that baby full of water, Dave was extremely relieved to see it hold water. It was a job well done "as unto the Lord."

Shifting to the third and final day of the school, it was time for the student ride-off, the time when they'd get to display the skills that they'd learned. The air was flowing with excitement as the students were forced to rise to the challenge set before them.

Quite often, this is the time when students make the formidable decision to pursue rodeo in all sincerity or mark rodeo off the list for their future. Explosive efforts from the students result in gallant attempts to make great rides or they result in phenomenal wrecks. The bullfighting students are usually saved until the end of the ride off. They are each paired up with another bullfighting student, and a bull is turned loose in the arena. The two students take turns distracting and outmaneuvering the bull as he charges them. This is definitely a full-contact sport, as air flights are unscheduled and the landing spot is never known.

During one of the bull-fighting sessions, a student left the fight and ran to some instructors at the fence. Another student was sent in as the bullfighter at the fence told the instructors that he was not going to take another step until he got his life right with Jesus Christ. After the instructors led the young man into a personal relationship with Jesus, he asked them, "What do I do now?" The two instructors were young in their walk with Jesus and were somewhat unsure about what to say. That's when one of them came and got me, as I was also at the school in the role of a bareback-riding instructor. While the other students were still in the arena with the bull on the hook (the bull was still in a fighting mood), the young bullfighter

DALE HIRSCHMAN

knelt by the fence while I visited with him about his next steps in following Jesus. As the conversation progressed, I shared with him about water baptism in obedience to God's Word. He asked, "When should I do it?"

"Right now if you want," was my response to him.

We've baptized people in water troughs, lakes, even a whirlpool in a locker room; so I figured that we'd find one of the above somewhere near. The young bullfighter was ready right then to get baptized, so I encouraged him to finish his bull fight, and I'd go find us a baptismal.

There was not a water trough anywhere in the back pens. I knew there was nothing large enough to dunk someone in at the gymnasium, so I asked Bronc if there was a pond nearby. There wasn't, and that's when Bronc pointed out this old bathtub in the ditch. I was astonished at how clean it was. The tub was on the short side of things, but I figured that God wouldn't mind if we hung their feet out the end of the tub.

As the final bullfight finished, Lyle allowed me to make an announcement with the old-fashioned PA system, suck in a lung full of air, and blast out, "We've had a young man receive Jesus, and he wishes to be baptized, so we're going to have a baptismal service over by the ditch, and you're invited to come if you want." People, estimated at around seventy of them, packed around the area as we started the baptism.

As the young man answered my questions, proclaiming Jesus as his Lord and Savior, the presence of God became so evident. No doubt rejoicing was going on in the spiritual realm. His baggy pants, suspenders, wild-colored shirt, and makeup all got wet as the bullfighter went under the cold, clear water on a Thanksgiving weekend.

A drenched, blessed man rose up out of the water to the crowd's applause. With handshakes and hugs, I turned to the crowd and made the offer for anyone else to get baptized if they never had and wanted to now.

Three other young men stepped out of the crowd to get baptized, one of whom was the son of an ordained minister who was a good friend of mine. *It was an awesome privilege to baptize this young man, as well as others, as his dad stood proudly by.*

The sun seemed to shine bright on that chilly, fall day as four soaked young men walked away closer to God than what they were when they came. I really don't think that they minded the cool air that much. A family was closer as they walked away together, and I was humbly blessed to be a part of it all.

One thing I was amazed at was how clean an old bathtub was outside at a rodeo arena. A year later, after returning to the next Sankey Thanksgiving Rodeo School, I learned about Dave and his ordeal of "doing things as unto the Lord." His obedience to stick to the task and finish a humiliating job was the groundwork for a move of God that changed lives for an eternity. Sometimes the things we do might seem trivial or unnecessary, but we never know how God is going to use us. Anytime we do things "as unto the Lord," God is using us to bring on a move of His power. We might not see the results right away or even in this lifetime, but rest assured God is using our efforts. What a mighty position to be in!

DALE HIRSCHMAN

THE COWBOY CALL

The Testimony

The spring of 1980 was the first time I stepped up and held a cowboy church service. I'm sure that if there are videos in heaven of things that happen on earth, then that first church service is more than likely in the bloopers section. However, the truth be known, the services I'm most proud of are probably in the bloopers section.

As the years have progressed, I have always tried to have different cowboys and cowgirls share their testimonies at the cowboy church services I've held. Unfortunately, there's not a lot of variety to the testimonies. Most are, "I was a bad boy, I mean a bad boy ... let me tell you how bad I was ..." Then he goes into the tale of how he did all the socially unacceptable sins. In several of the bad sins, you can discern a bit of bragging going on from the person, especially when he says, "I've been with women, lots of women." My flesh rises up, looking at who is talking, and I think, *Where did you find so many women that desperate?* I've never voiced that out loud yet.

One testimony that stands out above and beyond all the others is one shared by Gary Fike, a young bull rider from Panhandle State University, at the Weatherford, Oklahoma, college rodeo. As he started his testimony, he shared that as a young boy, he was in his home church when the pastor asked if anyone wanted to stand up and say, "Jesus is the Lord of my life, and I'm glad that He died for my sins." He expressed how he wanted to stand up and make the proclamation, but he never did follow through. As the pastor ended the opportunity, Gary shared how empty and disappointed he felt for not doing it.

Gary went on to share that he was never a hard partier, and he never had a drinking or drug problem; he was basically a good person. But he still needed Jesus and His

DALE HIRSCHMAN

forgiveness, for we all fall short of the glory of God. No one is without sin except Jesus. As Gary talked, it was nice to not hear all the sin stories and the evils. Gary spoke of his life story and how he received Jesus.

As he ended his testimony, he stated that he'd like to say one more thing. He paused, stood up straight in all confidence and assurance, held his head up, looked straight at the people, and then said, "Jesus Christ is Lord of my life, and I'm glad He died for my sins." He said a humble thank-you and sat down, a child of the most high God who was not ashamed of the gospel of Jesus Christ.

The Holy Ghost bumps shot up and down my whole body as I watched a man redeem himself for when he felt like he had missed God. Watching his stature and hearing his tone of voice as he spoke forth his proclamation of Jesus being his Lord has been burned into my heart and mind for an eternity. His testimony that day was living proof of the scripture found in Revelation 12:11, which says "They overcame him (the enemy) by the blood of the Lamb and the word of their testimony, and they loved not their life unto death."

Since that time I have shared Gary's testimony countless times at various church services. After sharing Gary's story, I've given people the opportunity to stand and make the same statement about Jesus that Gary did. It's not until we get to heaven that we will know how many lives have been touched from the encouragement they received to step up and testify.

At one service, a person told others for the first time ever that he had received Jesus as his Lord and Savior. Another time, a married couple, without knowing what the other was doing, both stood and simultaneously declared that Jesus was Lord of their lives and that they were glad that He died for their sins. We've seen young kids at junior rodeos stand and state their faith in Jesus. Watching the countenance on people's faces change to a glowing smile as they take a stand to testify for Jesus has and always will get my motor running.

Each and every person who knows Jesus as his or her personal Lord and Savior has a testimony to share. You might not have a wild, blood-and-guts testimony, which is a testimony in itself; but don't fail to share your testimony because you don't think it's exciting enough. You do not know whether or not your testimony might be the one that changes someone's life forever. The Word says that a word spoken in due season, how sweet it is. One thing is for sure: if you never share your testimony, it will never benefit anyone. So next time you get the chance to share, bow up, suck in some air, and let 'er rip for Jesus.

> Go home to your friends, and tell them what great things the Lord has done for you, and how He has had compassion on you.
>
> Mark 5:19 (NKJV)

> But sanctify the Lord God in your hearts, and always be ready to give a defense to everyone who asks you a reason for the hope that is in you, with meekness and fear.
>
> 1 Peter 3: 15 (NKJV)

> For we cannot but speak the things which we have seen and heard.
>
> Acts 4: 20 (NKJV)

DALE HIRSCHMAN

But His Word was in my heart like a burning fire, shut up in my bones; I was weary of holding it back, and I could not.

Jeremiah 20: 9b (NKJV)

The Call

As a young child, I grew up destined to be a cowboy.
While my older brother received cars and trucks for toys

when he was born, I was given toy horses, boots, and hats when I was born. No, this didn't make me a "cowboy"; but I do believe that this was a sign for things to come. Raised in a solid family with high standards in life, the only drug problem that I ever had was when my parents drug me to church every Sunday.

During one of those times when I was actually holding still in church, more or less, I heard the minister mention something about a horse. Of course, this got my attention and held it throughout the rest of the service. Hearing talk about a horse and even "cowboyin'" during a church service was about as common as hearing profanity in church—well, almost as common.

Our pastor had spent some time in Texas, pastoring a church, when he heard of a horse that two different horse trainers had been having problems breaking to ride. Our pastor saw this as a possible opportunity to witness to the community, so he took on the job of breaking the horse. As he stated, through love, prayer, and time, with great amounts of each, he finally managed to break the horse. As he finished his story, this thought ran through my head: *It would be neat to be a cowboy preacher.* To my conscious knowledge, the thought ran right on through my head without much interference.

As the years passed, I had the awesome privilege of pursuing my boyhood dreams, which lead me down the rodeo cowboy path. Running neck-to-neck with that path, I also grew stronger in my relationship with Jesus Christ. My rodeo career and my walk with Jesus both escalated during my life as a college student. The door opened for me to hold my first cowboy church service my senior year at a college rodeo. That church service was the start of the area of ministry I've been involved in ever since.

Two years after I graduated from college, I returned to become the assistant rodeo team coach and work on my master's degree. During that time span in college rodeo, if a person was enrolled in class, he/she could obtain a permit to compete in their home rodeo even if they had used all of their eligibility. That fit me to the tee. I entered every event that I thought I had even a minute chance of placing in: bareback riding, saddle bronc riding (my main events), bull riding (which I had retired from), and steer wrestling (which I had done a few times).

My fire had plenty of irons in it with being the assistant rodeo team coach, helping put on the rodeo, and competing every time the band played. One action-packed weekend started out with my bull ride first and ended with my bareback ride the last night. As the weekend rolled along, I tried my heart out each time I competed. I missed my steer in the steer wrestling but had ridden both my bronc and my bull. As the last night arrived, I was up in the bareback riding. The rodeo was a one go-round rodeo, so everyone got to compete once in whatever events they were entered in.

Bareback riding is a fast and furious eight seconds, starting with a nod of the head and ending only when you're on the ground and out of the way. It's a game of dish it out and take it. The horse blows in the air, kicks, and changes directions while you, the rider, drag your feet up the neck and then set them back in the horse's neck before he can start the next jump. Hesitation and timidity on the rider's part is a quick road to failure.

Not all horses have the timing (rhythm of bucking) that a cowboy desires and needs to make a good ride. Let me tell you, the horse that I was on that night was a *long* way from fitting in the desirable category. It was a battle from the git-go. I tried my best to make a good ride, but the horse couldn't decide which direction he wanted to go or what he was going to do while getting there, wherever "there" might have been for him. Finally, the whistle blew, and the pick-up men rode in and set me (thankfully) on the ground. I had fought with all my might, and I had won the battle with my opponent. The evening air flooded into my lungs again, my heart pulsated, adrenalin surged through my body, and I heard the rodeo announcer's voice booming through the airways.

DALE HIRSCHMAN

"This is Dale Hirschman, one of our cowboy preachers on the rodeo road today."

And time stood still as a boyhood thought, one that had been dormant for so long, raced through my head. *It would be neat to be a cowboy preacher.* I had been given the call, and now I was on that path. I realized the scripture, John 15:16, was evident in my life, "You did not choose Me but I chose you and appointed you that you should go and bear fruit, and that your fruit should remain" (NKJV).

Not everyone will receive or realize the call on their life in the same manner; but nevertheless, we all have a call on our lives as Jesus has given us the "ministry of reconciliation." We are Christ's ambassadors, God's representatives in whatever we do. A scripture that stood out to me when I was young in my walk with Jesus was, "Ye walk worthy of the vocation wherewith ye are called" (Ephesians 4:1b, KJV). I was pursuing the rodeo cowboy life when I really turned my life over to Jesus, so I tried my best to represent Him in my rodeoing.

In Proverbs 3:6 (NKJV), God tells us, "In all your ways acknowledge Him and He shall direct your paths." That means whatever our position in life, we are to represent Jesus in all that we do. Our call as Christians is to follow after Jesus every day of our lives. We each need to live our lives without hiding our relationship with Jesus.

One time, as I was traveling to a rodeo, I stopped at a gas station to grab a few items before going on to the arena. As I was trying to pay for the items, the cashier tried to make me pay for gas that I did not get. When I informed him that I wasn't the one with gas (which is rare, according to my wife) the cashier informed me that, yes, I was and I was going to pay for it. Now, I don't mind being a giving person and paying for someone else's gas if they're in need; however, I was not going to be told to pay for someone else's gas. (I know there is some pride in that last statement—more than what I want to admit.) As our "Yes, you did," "No, I didn't," conversation intensified, I didn't know if the cashier was about to come over the counter or not, and I was starting to hope he would. (I'm not the toughest guy around by any means, but he looked pretty soft. I think I could have taken him. If not, I know I could have outrun him.)

With the escalating disagreement in full swing, I finally looked at the man and said, "Look, Jesus Christ is Lord of my life, and I am to represent Him in all that I do. And I'm having a hard time doing that right now because I'm getting mad." The countenance and body posture of the man completely changed.

The angry tone left his voice as he stepped back and asked, "Who got the gas then?"

A lady who had just stepped out of the restroom replied, "I did."

The gentleman behind the counter and I exchanged apologies and "That's okays." I left the gas station dwelling on how sticking to representing Jesus changed the entire situation.

Not only are we to represent Jesus in all that we do, but we are to look for ways to minister to others in our circle of influence. As I've mentioned earlier, Jesus has given us the ministry of reconciliation. Reconciliation means "to bring back into harmony with." We are to do our best to bring others back into harmony with God. As we do that, we are walking out our call in life.

Power in the Blood

Many birthdays ago, after graduating from high school, my dad got me a job where he worked. The area where I worked required physical and mental strength because of the long hours and constant strain on the body. Each day at work was an endurance contest—a very well-paying endurance contest, I might add.

One day my dad walked by, stood in front of me, looked into my sweat-drenched face, and told me that my last name got me the job but I was the one who had to keep the job. It was an assembly line job, and I had to keep up with men who had been working for twenty to thirty years. During one day, as I found myself becoming fatigued and starting to fall behind, I started to sing one of my favorite songs from church, "Power in the Blood." I was in need of power, and that was what the song was about. As I started singing, I noticed that I was re-energized and I was able to keep up with the other workers.

Several years later, when I was holding cowboy church services, I shared my testimony of how God had renewed my strength when I started singing "Power in the Blood" while I was working. The next college rodeo season, a young bull rider shared a testimony of how he had been at the service and heard the "Power in the Blood" testimony.

A few months after the service, the young bull rider found himself going broke trying to rodeo; so he had to get a job. The young man found a job as a wheelbarrow jockey for a construction crew. If you're six foot two inches tall and weighing in at 235 pounds, pushing around a wheel-barrow full of sand, gravel, and concrete is not too much of a big deal; however, the bull rider was about seven inches shorter than that and around ninety pounds lighter. The wheelbarrow was getting heavier, and the terrain was getting rougher for the cowboy at his new job. As he was in one of those exhausted states, he remembered the "Power in the Blood" testimony. He started singing the song as he worked; and God, being true to His form,

DALE HIRSCHMAN

renewed the young man's strength. He was able to keep up with the work.

During one of the times the young man was singing, one of the workers approached him. "Boy, what are you singing?"

As the young bull rider looked up at the large, rough, foul-mouthed, crusty, old construction worker, he thought, *Oh no. This is it,* meaning the end of his life or worse. Summoning up his courage, he looked at the old man and said, "'Power in the Blood,' sir."

The old man stared at him for a second and then proclaimed, "Well, teach it to me, and I'll sing it with you."

By the end of the summer, the young bull rider led the old construction worker into a relationship with the King of kings, Jesus Christ.

But wait. There's more to this "Power in the Blood" testimony. Several years had passed, and I constantly shared the two testimonies of the "Power in the Blood" song. Stewart Hines, a student of mine from the school where I taught, was going with me to help with cowboy church services. He heard the two testimonies during one of the services. The next football season, Stewart, a running back, was in the middle of practice. The day was "maxing out day" in the weight room. With the entire high school football team gathered around as close as they could, Stewart was at the squat rack with 450 pounds on the bar. The permanent aroma of rotten socks dwelt in the air as the sweaty-bodied football players stood watching Stewart lower into the squatting position with the 450 pounds on his shoulders.

As the ascension of the weights began, Stewart stalled out. Nothing was budging. Standing there in the squatted position, Stewart's mind raced back to a testimony that he had heard; and in front of the entire football team, with their undivided attention, Stewart started singing out loud, "There is power, power, wonder-working power in the Blood of the Lamb, There is power…"

Stewart told me later, "Mr. Hirschman, the weights just started going up." The 450 pounds was the most anyone squatted for the entire football team that day.

The story of Stewart and "Power in the Blood" doesn't end in the weight room. I teach school in Clinton, Oklahoma, which has been declared the football capital of Oklahoma. Clinton High School has won numerous state championships in class 4A. Stewart's senior year found Clinton back in the state championship game as usual. The first series of plays ended with the other team basically just flat-out running over Clinton and punching the football into the end zone. Clinton received the kick-off, and four plays later, they were punting the football back to the opposing team. The next series of plays was looking a lot like the first series as the opposing team was driving the ball back down the field.

Stewart felt extremely lethargic during the first part of the game. Not knowing what to do to physically get back into the game, he turned his heart toward heaven and started singing out loud—you guessed it—"Power in the Blood." Stewart said that he never missed a block or a tackle the rest of the game, a game Clinton won. Can you imagine being on the football field and lining up across from a guy who, instead of calling you and your mother every foul name he can think of, is smiling and singing, "There is power, power, wonder-working power in the

Blood of the Lamb," and then he runs over you and helps you up, smiling the whole time?

It's not the words of a song that give us power; it's the fact that we are praising the Lord in the middle of our adversity. God inhabits the praises of His people. In Him, we live and move and have our being. He's the one who gives us strength to do what we need to do.

Does it mean that we'll win every football game or ride every bull if we sing "Power in the Blood" when we compete? No, because God knows the thoughts and intents of our hearts. He knows if we are doing it to manipulate Him or if we are doing it out of a pure heart for Him. Praising Him when we are in trouble is what He wants us to do. Praising Him when we are not in trouble is what He wants us to do. God wants us to praise Him, period.

There is the spiritual law of sowing and reaping. If we are sowing to the flesh and then praising God to get us out of reaping from the flesh, it's not going to work. God knows our hearts. If people think they can live lives of sin and then praise God so He'll get them out of trouble, they are deceived. If you are trying your best to live for Jesus and you get in a bind, offer up that sacrifice of praise unto the King of kings, and He will deliver you.

Look at Paul and Silas as they were in the bottom of the prison, locked up in chains, with their bodies sore and cut up from the beatings that they had received for setting a girl free from demons. At the midnight hour, they were singing praises and praying. The others in the prison could hear them. Paul and Silas were not in the "let's see who can sing the quietest" contest, which goes on in a lot of churches today. God miraculously freed them and saved the souls of an entire family. You can read the account in Acts 16:16–34.

Somewhere around the year 1979, I was entered in a college rodeo, getting ready to crawl down in the chute to get on a saddle bronc. A couple of weeks earlier, I had hurt my right knee, and it was still swollen to about the size of a cantaloupe. The bucking chutes were made of square tubing, and I eased down into my saddle. I tried to slide my injured right knee below the swells of the saddle, when the bronc just literally fell to the right side of the chute, pinning my knee between the swells of the saddle and one of the corners of the tubing. The pain was excruciating as the damaged knee took the blunt of the blow from the horse leaning. Those around me instantly went to pulling the horse off my leg. The horse turned into a total and complete idiot. He started trying to roll over on his side in the chute. He pawed the chute gate, trying to get some traction to get himself rolled over. The excruciating pain did something that I thought it couldn't do. It got worse. My knee was now taking not only his weight but the power from his shoving up against the chute.

Throughout the years of riding rough stock in rodeos, a person gets introduced to pain quite often; so you get used to it. I had been blessed with the ability to keep a clear head in the midst of a storm and to get out of the situations without panicking. However, this was by far the worst pain I had ever experienced. This irritation was pushing my limits on pain thresholds.

The more the cowboys around fought to get the horse off my leg, the more the horse fought to stay on my leg. There was no way anyone could have just picked the horse up, and there seemed to be no way to remedy the problem, short of shooting either me or the horse. The horse cost too much, so that put me in the limelight for taking the bullet. Thankfully, that was marked off the options list. However, my misery would have been over!

The steel tubing wasn't moving; the saddle wasn't moving in the right direction; and unfortunately, my leg wasn't moving either. My options of getting out of the worst pain I had ever experienced had just about run out. With my chute help exhausted from trying so hard to help, I didn't know what else to do, short of screaming and sliding into a state of total panic. That's when from inside me came forth praises to my God. The praises that were coming out of my mouth were not quiet little jabbering. Of course, they weren't elegant King James-type praises either. I started loudly saying, "Praise the Lord." Over and over, I said it.

Those around me stopped what they were doing and just stared at me. This was during a time when it wasn't cool to be a Christian cowboy or as common as it is today.

It would be neat to say that the horse levitated up off my leg or that he suddenly stood up, totally calm. Neither of those happened. What did happen was by far better. The pain just totally left. The horse was still on my leg, acting like an idiot, but the pain was gone. Calm came over me as I started working with the horse to get him up. Of course, the cowboys continued to stare at me.

Finally, we got the horse up. I slid into position and nodded my head. I would like to say that the horse really bucked and I rode great and won first. Reality, though, was that the horse was just as sorry outside of the chute as he was in the chute, and we only scored fifty-something. The outcome of the ride is trivial compared to the fact that God miraculously showed up in my dark hour when I turned to praising Him. My deliverance, Stewart's deliverance, Paul and Silas's deliverance, and a young bull rider's deliverance came when we looked past our problems and praised the Lord. So what are you waiting for? Praise the Lord.

> I will declare Your name to my brethren; In the midst of the assembly I will praise You.
>
> Psalm 22:22 (NKJV)

> But at midnight Paul and Silas were praying and singing hymns to God and the prisoners were listening to them.
>
> Acts 16:25 (NKJV)

DALE HIRSCHMAN

Your Best Shot

Even before I really dedicated my life to Jesus, I always knew that my artistic talents were a gift from God. Because of that, there were some things that I would simply not draw. I figured God gave me the talent so I would not dishonor Him by drawing inappropriate artwork. As good as that sounds to me, it doesn't mean that it sounds that good to everyone else.

That was the case for a friend of mine, who we'll call Rusty. It seems that Rusty had seen a drawing that instilled a heartfelt desire to have a copy of it. Maybe because I was the only artist that Rusty knew, he asked me to do the drawing for him. I've got to say that he was exceptionally excited as he described what he wanted me to draw for him. Needless to say, his mood swung to the other side of the pendulum when he heard my answer. Over and over, he tried to get me to change my stance on what subject matter I would draw, but to no avail; and he finally left.

Several months passed before Rusty and I crossed paths again. And when our paths did cross, Rusty would bring up the artwork request and try again to convince me to do the project for him. I do have to admit that Rusty's persistence was admirable, to say the least. The request, though, soon shifted from admirable to annoying. My bullheadedness was tested but not overcome by Rusty's bulldog tenacity.

There was a problem, though, that crept up. Rusty didn't mind having a drink or two, or three, or even four or more. When some people consume large amounts of "cool ones," they tend to develop a "nine feet tall and bulletproof" attitude. Rusty teeter-tottered in that stage. If I was around him when he had been drinking, he would start to bow up to me and try to threaten me to do the artwork for him. He never could push me into a fight; so he vented his frustrations at me for not fulfilling his request.

As was my way when handling intoxicated people, I would always talk my way out of an altercation until they

DALE HIRSCHMAN

would be distracted by something else, and I would take the opportunity to disappear out of sight. Out of sight, out of mind works exceptionally well with inebriated people. That was the way things went for several years until our paths crossed less and less.

Fast-forward several years to when I had just taken the position as assistant rodeo team coach for Southwestern Oklahoma State University in Weatherford, Oklahoma. We were into the spring season and starting our home rodeo, and I was under the spotlight to see if I could help produce what I thought to be the best college rodeo in the region. To put it mildly, we had been extremely busy getting everything ready. The first night of the rodeo had arrived, and I was running ninety miles an hour, trying my best to make sure that everything that I was responsible for was going slicker than snot on a doorknob.

During one of my umpteen times to make a trip around the bucking chutes area, I was passing by some of the parked vehicles out back when I heard someone call out my name. The parking area was dark, and the only light out there somewhat blinded me from seeing who it was; so I stopped and waited on the figure to come out of the shadows. Low and behold, the person who stepped out of the shadows was none other than Rusty; and he had a beer in each hand.

I was sociable as we continued on our way. He was very friendly, and it was good to visit with him, as it had been several years since I'd seen him. However, the pleasant conversation shifted as I noticed that each step that he took, his chest seemed to bow out more and more. He started his "yeah-yeahing" about the artwork and then stepped in front of me just when I was about to step through the gate into the arena. How he even got that far without being stopped by security for having the beer was a total shock. But he was there with a beer in each hand, his chest bowed out, getting more and more belligerent all the time. I had a rodeo to put on, and I did not have time to try to talk my way out of a fight. The likelihood of a fight was fantastic.

Here I was, a Christian cowboy who was not only vocal about my faith in Jesus but I had been holding cowboy church services at the college rodeos for quite some time. And now the situation looked like I was corralled into a fight at my home rodeo, in front of everybody. My adrenaline was pumping from working the rodeo; so I was pretty wired already, plus I was still rodeoing, so I was in good physical condition.

As he stood there, taking my costly time, I started surveying the situation. He had a beer in each hand, so that offered me the golden opportunity to bust him in the nose as hard as I could. I knew that even if he saw it coming, he would hesitate to block the blow because his beer was too precious to drop or take a chance at spilling. So I knew that my first lick was a freebie. As he talked, I no longer understood his words. I could feel the same sensation that would come over me the split second before I nodded my head in the bareback riding. It was the "let's get it on" mental mode. I could feel my mind clicking as I let 'er rip and hit Rusty with my absolute best shot.

I said to him, "Rusty, do you know that Jesus loves you?"

I could not have physically hit him any harder. His head immediately dropped, and his shoulders shrugged as his hands dropped to his side. (He still didn't spill his beer.)

DALE HIRSCHMAN

His answer was a sheepish, "Yeah. I know that," as he did not make eye contact with me anymore.

"Rusty, do you know that Jesus died for your sins?"

Another sheepish answer: "Yeah, I do. But, Dale, I've done a lot of bad stuff."

I assured Rusty that he hadn't done anything that Jesus wouldn't forgive him for if he would just ask Him to. I told Rusty again that Jesus loved him as I excused myself to the arena and said that I'd see him later. Even with the "see you later" statement, I never have seen Rusty again. If I would have given into the fleshly desire to fight him, then his last impression of me would have not been very constructive or encouraging; however, by following after the Holy Spirit, Rusty's last impression of me was one of me sharing the love of Jesus with him. You know it's always better to try to love someone into heaven than to try to beat the hell out of them.

The whole incident with Rusty only took a couple of minutes, but it burned into my heart for an eternity the power of the name of Jesus. Here was a volatile situation that was turned completely around by using the name of Jesus. The definition for the Greek word *name* literally means "authority." So when we use the name of Jesus, we are using the authority of Jesus.

In Philippians 2:9–11 (NKJV), the Bible says:

> Therefore God also has highly exalted Him and given Him the name which is above every name, that at the name of Jesus every knee should bow, of those in heaven, and those on earth, and of those under the earth, and that every tongue should confess that Jesus Christ is Lord, to the glory of God the Father.

Then in Mark 16:17–18 (NKJV), the Bible states:

> And these signs shall follow those who believe: In My name they will cast out demons; they will speak with new tongues; they will take up serpents; and if they drink anything deadly, it will by no means hurt them; they will lay hands on the sick, and they will recover.

We do these things listed above in the authority of Jesus, obviously not in our authority. That would be a total wreck if I tried to do any of that in my name alone. However, as we trust in Jesus, He gives us the power to do what He commands us to do.

The name of Jesus is so powerful that people have a hard time saying it unless it's in vain. I've never heard anyone use Buddha's or Allah's name in vain, only God's and Jesus's name.

The reason for that is that there is no power in the others' names. If you ever talk to someone who is not a Christian, they will not say the name of Jesus unless they are using it in vain.

As I've tried to witness or share with other people about Jesus and they say they are Christians but then they have a hard time saying the name of Jesus, this sends up a red flag on their spiritual wellbeing. This type of person is the type who is trusting in their "good ol' boy" status or their church membership for their salvation. First Corinthians 12:3b tells us, "No one can say that Jesus is Lord except by the Holy Spirit" (NKJV). If Jesus is your Lord, then call Him by His name: Jesus Christ.

After a college rodeo cowboy church service, I was rolling up sound system cords and visiting with a few people who were hanging around when I noticed an elderly cowboy standing back, obviously waiting for his turn to speak. I quickly put my equipment down and stepped toward him. This gentleman was adorned in his cowboy hat and a polyester suit from the late sixties. He was thin, almost frail-looking, as he stepped up to meet me.

He reached out his hand to shake, and I hate to admit it, but I was concerned about hurting him if I squeezed too hard. He held his head up in a dignified manner and spoke to me as he held onto my hand. He said, "Young man"—I appreciate that more and more as the years pass—"I perceive that you know Him." This elderly gentleman now had my full attention as he continued. He pointed toward the sky. "I perceive that you know Him, for you call Him by name."

And now I held on to his hand as he talked and I listened.

"You call Him by name, not 'the man upstairs' or the 'Good Lord' but by His name, Jesus."

He shuffled on by me as I stepped aside, realizing that I was in the presence of a man of God, for he called Him by His name.

What's the name of your Lord?

Victory Lap

My bout with Mid-States Rodeo Company's WNFR bareback horse, Joe Kidd, had just ended. I cheerfully listened to my name being placed on the top of the leader board with a score of 76 points.

With only two riders left in the evening performance, the arena director told me to go ahead and get on the victory lap horse that was directly behind the rodeo queen on her horse. The winner of each event takes a victory lap around the arena, following the rodeo queen, who is carrying the event sponsor's flag. I cannot stand to see a rodeo queen have to lope around because the winning cowboy can't ride a saddle-broke horse. As I stepped aboard the victory lap horse, I told the queen to not be afraid to "whup and spur" because I could ride a horse.

I was mounted up and ready to ride with just one cowboy left to compete in the bareback riding. I must admit that it did feel good to be on the victory lap horse. The last cowboy out was Hyde Kramer, and he had another WNFR horse called Bad Buddy. Eight seconds later, Hyde was also given 76 points. The arena director was hollering at the queen to lead off the victory lap as Hyde was rounding the corner of the gate. With no time to look for another horse for him to ride, he just stuck out his arm to me as I rode by. We grasped arms, and he swung aboard behind me. The queen's horse was already on the move, and away we went behind her.

The queen took me serious about "whupping and spurring," as we had to ride to catch up to her. We were blowing past the grandstands as the crowd did their respectful clapping as we rode by, tipping our hats. Rounding the far end of the arena, Hyde and I screwed our hats back on since there weren't any stands on the backside. I jokingly told Hyde to kick the horse in the flank to see if she'd buck. He quickly responded with a definite, "No."

Descending down the opposite side of the arena, we started our hat-tipping ritual as the crowd started their clapping ritual. Less than halfway down the arena, our horse's head disappeared in a flash. The split reins slipped through my hands like ripping line from a fishing reel. The saddle rammed back up under me as the paint mare blew into the air. I crammed my hat back on my head as I tried fruitlessly to pull that gal's head up so she would quit bucking. I was way too late to do that.

With me concentrating on my hat waving to the crowd, the paint lady buried her head between her front legs and was wholeheartedly committed to throwing a fit. She was taking advantage of her distracted jockeys. Now, I've seen similar situations where the victory lap horse "broke in two" and the champion cowboys piled onto the ground. Hyde was a "sure enough" ranch cowboy, and I was just too bullheaded to let that happen to us. Hyde reached forward with his feet and got a hold over my feet in the stirrups. He also had a hold on the cantle roll on the back of the cantle, and his chest bounced off my back as he bowed up to stick it on this bronc.

For the load that the mare was packin,' she really got it on.

She squalled and snorted as she blew in the air, circling around to the left. She would have really been a handful with only one rider on her. I could hear the crowd roaring as the Wild West exhibition was taking place out in the arena. She got with it for at least five or six seconds before she finally stopped.

She stood, her legs in a stiff, wide stance and her head down; and she was quivering like a leaf. I knew if I tugged any at all on the reins that she would possibly flip straight over backward. I dropped my rein hand on her neck and drummed her in the belly with my feet. The saddle blew vertical in the mix of squealing and bawling—the horse, not us. The real bronc ride was on again. The crowd was going nuts again. Neither Hyde nor I had weakened, and the mare sure was trying us; but this time, she got winded quicker, and she shut it down.

She was standing there, quivering and locked up as mad as a hornet.

Hyde told me, "She's just going to keep doing this. I'm getting off."

With that, Hyde bailed off the back. Round number three erupted with the sudden loss of weight. The pretty painted pony went to jumping and blowing in the air again. I snatched her head up and drilled her in the belly again. She left the bronc fit and broke into a hard run. I rode her across the arena and out the gate with a tip of my hat to the roaring of the crowd. The crowd celebrated that accidental bronc ride more than any planned part of the rodeo that night. My adrenaline was surging through me. We had topped off the bronc, and I rode out of the arena, looking and feeling like a hero.

DALE HIRSCHMAN

Looking back, that night was one of the highlights of my rodeo career. The cool evening, crowd, and winning a check in the bareback riding were tremendous; but the victory lap was by far the part burned into my memory. Events like the victory lap are what I miss when I think of the old rodeoing days. But I realize that I have not made my final victory lap.

One day it will be time to mount up with the King of kings and the Lord of lords. On that day, when I will get to take part in the armies of heaven who are mounted up on white horses, I can see in my mind that my horse will be a big, square-bodied horse. His full mane will flow out of and hang on both sides of a big, thick neck, one that will take up my whole palm as I clamp down on the top of it. Where his massive neck connects to his head will be a thick, stout jaw. His eyes will be wide and full of excitement, anxious, hardly being able to wait to go. The rollers will be going in his flared nostrils as he'll be snorting, blowing, and pacing about. The veins on his head will be bulging. His forelock will be full and long, past the end of his roman nose, almost covering his eyes on both sides. His shoulders will be waves of rippling muscles. His withers will be a solid, good size. He definitely will not be mutton-withered. His big, solid, squared chest will flow into his muscled forearms that have the bulging veins cascading up and down his legs. His feathered fetlocks will hang halfway down his hooves. His heart girth will be deep and full, running back to an enormously muscled rear end. Last but not least, he'll have a kink thrown into his long, flowing tail. When that day comes, I'll recognize him when I see him, and I bet he'll recognize me too.

Now I saw heaven opened, and behold, a white horse. And He who sat on him was called Faithful and True, and in righteousness He judges and makes war. His eyes were like a flame of fire and on His head were many crowns. He had a name written that no one knew except Himself. He was clothed with a robe dipped in blood, and His name is called The Word of God. And the armies in heaven clothed in fine linen, white and clean followed Him on white horses!

Revelations 19:11–14 (NKJV)

DALE HIRSCHMAN

THE COWBOY CALL

Hail No

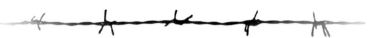

One April, while I was traveling north out of Canadian, Texas, I ran into a little adverse weather. The sky went to dumping loads of pea-sized hail on me, my pickup, and everything around us. Most hail storms near my home fires come more in spurts, but this one just kept coming down. The hailstones started drifting across the road, causing my driving speed to slow down to a crawling thirty-five miles per hour. As my pickup took a pounding by the constant barrage of hail, I really wasn't worried about any hail damage. I figured that any new hail damage would just blend in with the old hail damage.

The land around me was mainly wheat pasture and home to a lot of stocker cattle. The steers on the wheat were bunched up, packed together, and wadded up about as tight as they could get while each of them were headed down wind of the hail.

As I crept along through the hailstorm, I noticed one steer standing away from the herd. He was cold, wet, and getting pelted from the hail. As I drove by, watching this poor creature, God spoke to me.

"That's a Christian out of fellowship."

DALE HIRSCHMAN

As my eyes scanned the herd of bunched-up, hump-backed, head-lowered steers, I noticed that all the steers were being affected by the hail. The ones on the outer edges of the herd were getting hit along one side and on the top of their backs. Their other side was being protected by being pressed up against another steer. The steers in the inner core of the herd were hit by hail, but only a small part of their backs were in the strike zone. In fact, some were still relatively dry because the rest of their body was totally surrounded by the other steers.

We, as Christians, are like those steers. We all catch a little hail in our lives. We all have trials and tribulations. However, like the steers in the middle of the herd, the deeper we are in fellowship with Jesus and other believers, the less effect the hail has on us. The farther away from the center of fellowship we get, the more we are exposed to getting pelted by the storms of life. When we get totally out of fellowship with Jesus and other believers, we are completely exposed to the storms of life, and we catch hail from all directions.

Predators in the natural world attack an animal that is away from the herd because that is when they are in their weakest state, even though they might still be physically strong. When we get away from our relationship with our heavenly Father and other Christians, we place ourselves in a spot for greater attacks from our enemy, the devil. Even though we might be spiritually strong at the start, we will weaken if we are out of fellowship. The days of the Lone Ranger are over. Besides, he even had Tonto.

Group Participation

During the latter half of my college rodeo days, I had the privilege to haul to the rodeos with our rodeo team coaches, Dr. Don Mitchell and Barry Davis. Since that time, Barry has gone home to be with Jesus, but Doc is alive and kickin' while he enjoys ranching with his wife. I have the highest respect for both men, for their integrity and their commitment to the rodeo team. They worked hard and put in long hours for the team's success in and out of the arena. Both men were solid foundations for a lot of flighty college students who were trying to settle into a direction in life and rodeo and get an education.

During one of the road trips back from a college rodeo, I got to witness Doc and Barry's protective attitude toward their team members. On the outskirts of Woodward, Oklahoma, a carload of idiots tried to run some of the pickups with trailers off the road. The car would cut in front of the pickups and slow down and then weave back and forth in front of them. We were behind the pickups; and in no time, Doc had whipped around them and pulled up behind the car. The car pulled over into an empty parking lot after a barrage of Doc flashing his lights at them.

Doc pulled up beside the other vehicle and proceeded to instruct the driver about driving etiquette. The other driver did not have much response to the verbal tongue lashing that he was taking. When a person is arguing with someone who is not only smarter but also in the right, it's hard to hold up his end of the argument. So the other person just sat there and took it.

Finally, out of desperation, the driver's girlfriend shouted out at Doc, "My boyfriend doesn't like the way you're talking to him."

Now, it wasn't a great response, but it was at least a response.

By this time, Doc was hot enough under the collar that I could see his ears glowing red.

Doc answered the young lady with, "Well, just tell your boyfriend to get out of the car if he doesn't like it."

Right at that instant, Barry unlatched his door but held it shut so the cab light wouldn't come on. Oh man! I went to emptying my pockets of everything that I didn't want messed up 'cause I knew that if that guy in the other car made the mistake of getting out, then the fight would be on! And I knew that it would be group participation night. Both Doc and Barry had been in their share of scrapes, and their unwritten resume in the rear-kickin' department was good enough for most situations. I had no doubt that if anything erupted, I was on the overcoming side; however, I also knew that there would be no sitting on the sidelines, should the cars empty out.

There is a fine line between bravery and stupidity, and the driver of the other car chose not to cross that line as he sped off into the night. However, if he had chosen to take the giant leap and get out of the car, I knew that anything less than total group participation was not an option.

DALE HIRSCHMAN

Too often in today's church, the belief is just the opposite. People believe that it's just one man's job or the job of a chosen few to do all the ministering. The Word of God doesn't agree with this misconception.

Ephesians 4:11–12 (NKJV) states, "And He Himself gave some to be apostles, some prophets, some evangelists, and some pastors and teachers, for the equipping of the saints for the work of the ministry, for the edifying of the body of Christ."

Those who are in authority over us in the faith are not there to do all the work themselves, but they are there to prepare us to do the work of the ministry. We who have trusted Jesus as our Lord and Savior are the body of Christ, and we are to function as His body, doing His work here on this earth. We are not to sit in the pickup and watch as the battle rages on.

Part of the problem of Christians not getting involved is that they don't want to get their hands dirty or, heaven forbid, break a nail. In other words, some are just way too comfortable to get into the battle.

Not long ago, I received a phone call from a person that I had met briefly at a cowboy church service. The person on the phone informed me that he was stranded and had run out of money, equaling no food. He was near a church that I believed was turned on to Jesus and doing His work. I gave the individual their phone number and assured him that they would be there for him.

Time had rolled by before I heard from him again. In fact, I thought that the situation had been worked out when I received another phone call from him. His situation was not resolved, but a little worse. He had forgotten the name of the church and had been surviving by getting food from some people at a nearby bar. I gave him the name of the church and reassured him again that they would help him.

After some thought, I decided to call the church and give them the heads-up that he might be calling and to let them know of his predicament. That was when I got the bombshell. They had no programs to help the poor. They did not have a food bank, clothing storage, or even the desire to go check on this person who was stranded just three miles from their plush offices.

I realize that a church cannot just give out money or food to everyone who walks up and asks for it. But when one ministry calls to let them know of a person who is sincerely in a bind, and they will not leave their office to drive a short distance to investigate, there is a definite problem with their policies.

After spending a good part of two days trying to find someone to help and getting nowhere, I was aggravated, to put things mildly. During another phone call to the church, I asked them if they thought it was a good idea for me to drive seventy miles one way to check on this person who was three miles from them. The response was, "Yes. That sounds good to me."

I drove home from work, making plans to drive the 140-mile round trip the next day. I was shocked, angered, and repulsed at the lack of response from the churches I called to help the poor. Scriptures about helping the poor run rampant throughout the Bible. How could they be ignored?

On my way home, I made a quick little detour, exiting off the interstate on a country road. On the corner of the exit stood a man wearing a camouflage coat, with his dog and backpack beside him. In his hand was a cardboard sign that read, "Stranded." It is hard to avoid eye contact when there are only two people out in the country; but force of habit took over and I looked away, as I was conditioned to do. Driving away, I watched the man in my rearview. Many of those with cardboard signs standing on street corners have a concrete, statue posture, cold and emotionless. I watched this man's reaction as I drove away. It was not one of a cold concrete statue. His shoulders slumped as he dropped his sign to his side and stared at the ground. "No," jumped through my spirit. I was not going to turn my back on the poor.

I turned my pickup around and headed back. When I pulled up to him, I called him over to my pickup. He came to the pickup very tentatively and cautiously. I apologized to him for not being able to take him where he needed to go. His whole countenance changed, as he replied that it was okay. I shared with him that Jesus loved him and knew of his needs and that God knows how he spends his money so he better spend it wisely to take care of himself and his dog. With that, I slipped him some money and drove off. His posture was vastly improved as I watched him in the rearview mirror. My trip home was finished without any further alterations to my normal plans.

I am not going to give money to every person I see holding a cardboard sign. That would be foolish. However, I will be more sensitive to the Holy Spirit on who to give to. There are other creative ways to help: gift certificates to restaurants, food, or maybe a jacket or other clothing. The main thing is to not turn our backs on those in need.

The next day found me and a good friend headed to Oklahoma City with a load of food and clothes for my stranded acquaintance. We found the trailer where he was staying and dropped off the supplies for him and his friend. The way he was rejected by the area church made it hard to tell him that Jesus loves him, but he was receptive to it, as he had accepted Jesus as his Lord and Savior the year before. After getting the details of when their boss would return to get them and knowing they were set until he got there, we headed home.

We do not know all the reasons why some things happen the way they do. I do not know why no one close would help, but I do know that God worked some things in my life through those circumstances. There is a new determination in me to be sensitive to the leading of the Holy Spirit in helping others. I do not want to turn my back on the poor again.

I hope when you joined the family of Jesus Christ you didn't do it to sit on your rear and watch. In this family, group participation is not an option.

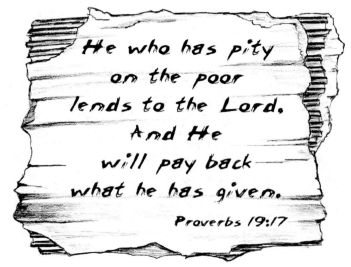

He who has pity
on the poor
lends to the Lord.
And He
will pay back
what he has given.

Proverbs 19:17

DALE HIRSCHMAN

Oklahoma Grizzlies

Several moons ago—in fact, a lot of moons ago—back to the college days to be exact, there was a group of about ten people who decided to make an excursion to the bat caves in Corn, Oklahoma. I was a member of that group. Most of the homies I ran with were of the redneck or country variety. Of this group, only two of its members could qualify as country-type people: me and one other cowboy. The others were city, born and raised. Several were paired with their boyfriend or girlfriend, out taking a romantic walk in the country.

The bat caves were located in a rancher's pasture, about a half a mile from where we had to park our vehicles: my pickup and their cars. The majority of the pasture road was actually an oil field road that was graveled. The others seemed to appreciate the graveled road because it kept the grass from tickling their legs, as they wore shorts out into the pasture.

After about one hundred yards of walking down this gravel road, I'd had about as much of a romantic, peaceful walk out in the country as I could stand. Where and with whom I was raised, a walk in the country always turned into a running, wrestling, rock-throwing, mud-slinging, goosing, and scaring time. My thought was, *Why should this walk be any different?* As I started drifting to the back of the herd of people, I scoped out the situation, studying just how I could turn this into a fun walk.

The sides of this gravel, oil field road were covered with tall Johnson grass and buffalo grass. Visibility into the side of the road was not very far. Just ahead on the road, I spied a rock about the size of a soccer ball. My plans to liven this walk up were becoming very plain to me. Bringing up the rear of this group, no one saw me pick

DALE HIRSCHMAN

up this large rock. I hoisted the rock over my head with both hands and heaved that baby into the grass beside the road. There was a good enough decline in the road that the old rock just bounced and ripped through the grass as it ran alongside our passageway. Everybody in the group leaped both vertically and horizontally when the unidentified object made such a ruckus in the tall grass! It looked like a synchronized stampede. I didn't think that a group of people could leap that high and go that far in the same split second—well, almost everyone. There was one young lady who, when the rock went tearing through the terrain, didn't jump like everyone else. The rock's unannounced landing was about two feet behind her and about five feet beside her and her boyfriend. As it traveled by, the girl jerked her arms up tight to her body and let out this blood-curdling scream, a scream that just kept going and going and going. Her body never moved except for a horrific trembling. Finally, the screaming simmered down to sobbing and then to crying. Even the quaking of her body slowed down to quivering as she stood there and cried. Her boyfriend, who was right beside her, came back to her and tried to console her as he gave me one of those "I'm a man, and I don't like what you did" looks.

Now, all I wanted to do was break the monotony of the walk in the country, but this was ridiculous (which they probably thought too). I wondered why in the world in western Oklahoma anyone would get that scared. What was she thinking it might have been, an Oklahoma grizzly bear? None had been seen in the state since the 1800s, if any were seen then. Or maybe she thought it was an African lion or some other mysterious thing. Whatever she thought it was, it sure scared her.

The rest of the trip was not near as eventful as the first of it was. I calmed down, and so did they. I spent most of my bat cave exploring by myself. I'm not sure, but I think some of them were more afraid of me than the bats flying around. At least I noticed that they kept an eye on me as much as possible.

Years later, I got to thinking about that girl's reaction to my entertaining rock throw. I realized how paralyzing fear can be. The girl was so gripped by fear that she could not move even when she thought she was in danger. Fear will cause people to hold back when they should be moving.

Look at 1 Samuel 17:1–16. Here, the Philistines and the Israelites were camped on mountain sides with a valley in between them; and every day, the Philistine champion, Goliath, came out and defiled the armies of Israel. The Israelites shrunk back in fear when Goliath stepped out to do his trash-talking. For forty days, every morning and every evening, Goliath stepped out and talked his smack. For forty days, the Israelites jumped back in fear.

Have you ever wondered why the Philistines didn't just go ahead and attack the Israelites? Basing my opinion on the fact that the Philistines cut a trail when their ace-in-the-hole, Goliath, lost his head in the heat of battle, I believe that the Philistines did not attack the Israelites was because they knew that they could not defeat them. The Israelites did not attack the Philistines because they did not think that they could defeat them. Fear hindered the Israelites from experiencing or even seeing the victory that was before them. Until their fear, Goliath, was removed, they did absolutely nothing. Our enemy, the devil, knows that he is a defeated foe; yet he also knows that if he can get people bound up in fear, then they will not exercise their authority. When the enemy attacks, fear is his point man. Fear is the first thing that he comes with as he charges into people's lives. When people first hear the word *cancer*, immediately, a wave of fear swarms them, usually rendering them useless and inactive in the spiritual realm. That is why it is so important to bind a spirit of fear when praying for someone's healing, for sure if it's a healing of cancer. After that, pray for God's peace to flood them, replacing the fear.

Throughout the years, I've seen cowboys who were coming back from an injury or who were getting older, and they hesitated when they should have been making a move during a bronc or bull ride. That hesitation usually caused a buck-off at the least or another injury. Fear will cause that slowed reaction, which, in the rodeo world, will bring failure and/or injury. In my later years of rodeoing, I noticed that there was one common denominator with all my injuries. Every time I was injured, I had let fear or disobedience enter into the situation.

One of those times was in Abilene, Texas, at the Texas Cowboy Rodeo Association Finals. I had qualified in both the bareback and the saddle bronc riding. The finals had gone okay, as I had placed in the bareback riding but not in the bronc riding. The last day of the finals had arrived; and Sarah, my wife, had flown down to be with me there in Abilene. I picked her up at the Abilene airport, and we drove straight to the arena, which was on the same side of town as the airport.

The rodeo went downhill pretty doggone quick for me that night. My bareback horse made one jump before turning to leave the chute and then blew out of there and made a major swoop to the left. There was no kick, and the horse just slapped me on the ground. Not only was it a cheap shot, but it rattled my brain just a hair. He never really fouled me, so there was no option for a re-ride. I just had to wait for the bronc riding.

The bronc riding came soon enough, and I was crawling back down into the chutes again. The bronc that I had I didn't really know, but I heard that he wanted to throw a guy off over his head. That style of bucking was countered by the bronc rider really lifting on his rein and setting his feet, which you should do anyway. However, I drifted more toward the reef and pull on the rein style. I know that pulling is not good in the bronc riding, but that's what I often did. Now I had a horse that a person really needed to lift on a lot, and I realized that he probably didn't fit my style.

As I nodded my head, I allowed a little fear to set in, and I hesitated. For the second time that evening, I got slammed into the ground, only this time I hit the ground with my elbow and snapped my head to the side. The lights went out all over the stadium—well, at least for me. With my world totally dark and a large buzzing going on in my head, everything was feeling pretty numb as I laid there in a heap on the arena floor.

The way I was raised, you did not lay there. You got up and got out of the arena. Everything inside of me was yelling, "Get up!" But my arms weren't cooperating. I would push myself up to my hands and knees, and then my arms would collapse. I remember my face helplessly driving itself into the ground, and everything inside of me started screaming again, "Get up! Get up!" After the third time of my face hitting the dirt, somebody got to me to

DALE HIRSCHMAN

help me up. I'm sure it was quite humorous to watch me flopping around in the arena, trying to stand up. With the help, I was able to get to my feet and start out of the arena. I only remember taking a couple of steps though.

My wife, who had never seen me hurt in the arena before, was watching the whole process quite intently. She told me that I took a couple of steps, and then my toes turned in and drug two furrows through the dirt as I was helped out of the arena as the announcer said, "Let's give Dale a hand as he leaves the arena under his own power."

My wits came back as I remember being leaned up against the fence in the alleyway. Unfortunately, I had been in this predicament before, and I knew what was going on. As I looked around me, there sat Kelly McCloy on her horse in the alley next to me. The air around me started getting real thin, and the world started spinning. I reached out and grabbed what I thought was the stirrup leathers on her saddle and held on tight to stabilize myself. (I found out later that I grabbed the calf of her leg and was about to tear it off.) As I held on, I told her not to leave me because I was about to pass out. She leaned over in her saddle and said, "I ain't leaving you, and you ain't passing out." I took another breath, and the O_2 level in my head went up. I told Kelly that I was going over to my gear bag, and if she saw me anywhere else she was to send me back to my gear bag.

When I arrived at my gear bag, I realized that I needed my saddle; so I told the guys by my gear bag I was going to get my saddle and if they saw me anywhere else to send me back to my gear bag. I realize that telling others of my plans and putting someone in charge of me sounds silly, but I was having a hard time maintaining consciousness and focusing on the task at hand. I had to constantly tell myself what I was doing, where I was going, and to keep breathing. At the same time, I was rebuking Satan and his attacks on me in the name of Jesus.

Finally, I was ready to go see Sarah and talk to her. I really had to concentrate and fight down any anxiety and panic as I made the several turns up the steps and hallway to the stands. There were only two or three turns that I had to make; but with each one, I had to fight to keep from losing my equilibrium and sense of direction.

After we met and talked, a friend of mine, Terry Wenetschlaeger, came up and told us that he'd take me and help me get the dirt washed off my face before Sarah and I left. I hadn't realized that my face was covered with dirt. Go figure. Terry led me out of the coliseum and to a horse barn next door that had a large restroom where I could clean up. For the first time that evening, the numbness started wearing off, and pain and fatigue started setting in. As I was cleaning up, I had to sit down and rest. I was becoming extremely weary.

With any injury in a sport, a person has the temptation to wonder if the cost is worth it to continue in that sport, and I was no exception. The thoughts of "hanging up the spurs" and quitting rodeo had crossed my mind more than once that evening!

As I sat there Fred Pitts, a Jesus-loving stock contractor, showed up in that horse barn restroom. I don't know how he found us, but he did. He stood there, tall and lanky, with his high top buckaroo boots on and his handlebar moustache. Then he said to me, "Dale Hirschman, God don't want you to quit." Fred said some more things, but that first line jumped into my Spirit as

I sat there and listened to him. Fred finished his mission from God, Terry finished helping me get cleaned up, and off to Sarah we went.

Now we were faced with a new obstacle. Sarah had flown in and didn't know how to get out of town, and I couldn't remember. It was dark, and neither of us knew what direction to go in. When we left the parking lot, we made a few turns, and then I couldn't even tell you which way was north or south. Sarah didn't know either, so we drove until we saw a motel, and we got a room. After camping out in the motel room, we woke up to a bright, shining sun; and my head was on straight again, so we headed home. All of that struggle because I let fear slip into my life within just a split second time frame.

Fear is the fruit of doubt. Fear is opposite of faith. Faith took Joshua and Caleb into the promised land. Fear and doubt kept the other Israelites out. Fear is not being totally convinced that God can take care of the situation you are in. Fear is the result of not being close in your relationship with God. "Perfect love casts out fear" (1 John 4:18, NKJV). The closer we get to God's perfect love, the more fear is driven out of our lives. Fear can't hang with God. "For God has not given us the spirit of fear, but of power, and of love, and a sound mind" (2 Timothy 1:7, NKJV). Fear cripples us in our witness for Jesus. It's not from God, so we don't have to have it.

Several years before the Abilene episode, I had been battling fear on a regular basis, and I was at a home Bible study one night where the teacher taught on the subject of fear. It was a pretty laid-back type of night, and at the end of the Bible study, the teacher asked nonchalantly if anyone was having problems with fear and wanted deliverance from it. Shucks. I had been having some problems with fear, and I thought, *Sure, I want free from fear.* I jumped up for prayer, and then the Holy Spirit showed up. The preacher barely touched me, and the Holy Spirit fell upon me. In the book of 1 Kings 8:11, it talks about how the priests were unable to stand to minister because of the cloud (presence of God) that was there. I've seen people slain in the Spirit before, so that wasn't anything new to me; however, this time it was me, and I hit the ground like a rock. I wasn't expecting God to knock me off my feet, but He sure did. My knees buckled, and down I went. I laid there for a while, not being able to stand back up and not wanting to either. I felt a little lighter as I got up, but not much different.

Several weeks had passed when I noticed that not much was bothering me, not any of the bareback horses that I was getting on at rodeos or anything for that matter. I realized that I was delivered from fear.

DALE HIRSCHMAN

Have I ever battled the temptation of fear since then? Yes, but it hasn't had a hold on me like it did before that night at the home Bible study. I learned how much I was set free from fear just a month or so from that deliverance night. I was single at the time and shared a small apartment with a friend of mine. We had an unspoken courtesy that if one of us came in real late at night, we would turn on a light in the apartment just to let the other one know that we were home. One weekend, my roommate left for his home, and I stayed in the apartment that weekend. After an exhausting day Friday, I crashed in bed and was out before my head hit the pillow, figuratively speaking, of course.

Sometime in the night, I heard something from the living room of our apartment. As I strained to focus my blurred vision toward the sound, I saw the silhouette of a person sneaking across the living room. I knew that if it was my roommate, he would have turned on a light. That meant I had someone prowling around in my apartment. Not only that, but I was mega tired too. When faced with a major challenge, I did what we should always do. I prayed. I prayed, *God, there's someone in our house, and I'm tired. You take care of this one, okay? I'm going back to sleep,* which I did, even with someone stalking around in my apartment. And I slept peacefully too.

I found out that following Monday that the prowler in my apartment was my roommate. For some reason, that time, he did not turn on a light. I did not know it was him that Friday night; but it did not matter because, "If God is for us who can be against us?" (Romans 8:31b, NKJV). Besides that, "God has not given us a spirit of fear, but of power, and of love and a sound mind," (2 Timothy 1:7, NKJV). So, if you're faced with a fear as big as a Goliath or an Oklahoma grizzly, realize that they are not from God, and you don't have to be hindered or held back because of them.

DALE HIRSCHMAN

The Desires of Your Heart

July 1971 found my family on the front row of the grandstands at the Cheyenne Frontier Days Rodeo in Cheyenne, Wyoming. I absorbed every bit of the action that I could. I would not have been surprised if a vacuum sound could be heard as the visual images were being pulled into my soul with my eyes. As a veteran of a few twelve-years-old-and-under miniature rodeos, I already knew that I was destined to be a rodeo cowboy. The seed to compete in the Cheyenne Frontier Days was embedded in my life on that cool July day.

Years passed as my walk with Jesus and my rodeo career grew. Hauling with another Jesus-loving cowboy, Marty Cummins, brought us to a visit with Marty's grandparents. Marty's grandparents were pastors of a small country church, and they were sold out to Jesus like no one else I had ever met. We spent several days at their place, and his grandparents were bombarded with questions concerning the Bible. During one of the question-and-answer sessions, I asked Marty's grandmother what Psalm 37:4 (NIV) meant. After I read it to her, she told me to read it again; so I did. "Delight yourself in the Lord and He will give you the desires of your heart."

She looked at me and replied, "That's what it means." I guess I had a blank stare because she came back with, "What it said is what it means." I was almost in shock that the meaning was so simple. The Bible means what it says. I was expecting a deep, profound interpretation that I really couldn't understand but wasn't willing to admit it because I didn't want to look stupid. I didn't exactly know what it meant to "delight yourself in the Lord," but I figured if I did my best to please Him, then He would probably give me the desires of my heart. And right then,

DALE HIRSCHMAN

during the early summer of 1981, my desire was to compete in the Cheyenne Frontier Days.

For most cowboys who fill their permits, which enables them full membership in the Professional Rodeo Cowboys Association, their desire is to pursue rookie of the year honors; but that wasn't a concern for me. My family had suffered the loss of my dad, and the last few years had been rocky for me, to say the least. I was on my own and just regaining the motivation to be aggressive and try hard again. Finances were slim, and rodeoing was on a limited basis for me. The month of June went well as I picked up a few checks, making the goal of being able to enter Cheyenne a reality. For some airhead reason, that year, entries for Cheyenne had to be paid a month early.

I entered both the bareback and saddle bronc riding, so my entry fees came to a grand total of almost everything in my checking account. After depleting my checking account for the fees at Cheyenne, rodeoing in the month of July went totally dry. I won zilch, nada, nothing! I was up at Cheyenne during the middle of the week, so I had two weekends left before I headed north. I pulled all my money from what was left in my checking account, savings account, and spare change jar. The total came up to just a hair over $17.00. The $17.00 fell short of being able to cover the cost of food and travel to Cheyenne, let alone any expenses that I accrued before leaving for Cheyenne. I had been rodeoing some with Marty, but now I couldn't enter anything!

The entire time of my financial challenges, I kept standing in faith on the promise of God that as "I delighted myself in Him, He would give me the desires of my heart." The first Sunday of the last two weekends before departure to Cheyenne, I went up front during church for special prayer. I did not disclose my desires to anyone because when my need was met, I wanted to know that it was God's doing, not someone acting on emotion. During the prayer time, God spoke to me. I know that some people have a problem with the "God told me" statement, which, quite often, I do too because some people abuse that statement way too much. However, this time, God told me my brothers wouldn't let me down.

I immediately knew that God had spoken to someone, and they were going to give me the money I needed. As church was over, sure enough, no one gave me anything. Monday came and went, and no money. Tuesday was the same as Monday. Wednesday was the same as Tuesday. "Your brothers won't let you down" was stirring in my spirit all through Wednesday night church, but I walked away with my need not met. Thursday morning arrived with me feeling pretty doggone hopeless. I didn't want to hitchhike all the way to Cheyenne. Nor did I want to go without eating for several days. And I for sure didn't want to stay at home.

Thursday evening, I received a phone call from Marty. He went right into talking about the horse that he had at the rodeo in Great Bend, KS. He didn't know it, but the conversation was like pouring salt into an open wound. Earlier, we had talked briefly about both of us entering Great Bend; but with no money, I didn't enter. Dell Hall had the rodeo; and Marty was excited about the good horse that he had drawn from the Dell Hall herd. Most of them in his pen were good son of a guns.

As we were bringing the conversation to a close, Marty asked, "What horse do you have?"

DALE HIRSCHMAN

Feeling a little ashamed that I hadn't entered, I informed Marty that I wasn't going.

"You have to. I entered you, and we're up Saturday night," was the reply that came through the phone lines.

Immediately, "Your brothers won't let you down," raced through my mind.

"Marty, let me call you right back. I need to call PROCOM."

PROCOM was the central entry office for the PRCA rodeos. I hung up the phone and started dialing the 800 number to PROCOM, and a lump was already rising up in my throat.

It took forever for PROCOM to answer. It took forever for me to give my membership number. It took forever for the operator to look up the rodeo. All the while, "Your brothers won't let you down," pulsated through my head.

"Sir, you have horse Number Ten Companion of the Rafter H Rodeo Company," was the operator's reply.

I thanked the operator and hung up the phone.

Number Ten Companion was selected to go the National Finals Rodeo multiple times. He was as honest a horse as you could possibly want. He started out really nice and would get stronger and stronger every jump. His bucking pattern was to circle around to the left. The tighter his circle, the stronger and higher he would get. If he circled tight, it felt like the whole world was dropping out from underneath you. He was a really good horse to get on, but he was no day off. He had ripped the riggin' out of the hand of several good cowboys.

Back to the lump in my throat that I had mentioned earlier. It just about leaped out when I received the livestock information. I called Marty back and informed him of my draw and my financial condition. No problem. He'd cover the finances until after they wrote the checks at the rodeo. I just had to take care of my part, riding Number Ten Companion.

On the way to the rodeo that Saturday, I was thinking that I needed the $75 that I borrowed from Marty, plus I guessed $500 for the trip to Cheyenne. I found out later that it would not take anywhere near the $500 for the trip to Cheyenne, but $500 sounded good to me.

DALE HIRSCHMAN

Arrival at the rodeo was just as typical as all the others. The same pre-rodeo rituals: taping, stretching, and telling Wild West stories all while mentally visualizing the upcoming conflict with the bucking horse. My evening was outwardly the same as usual; but inwardly, things were different. This would be my third time getting on Companion. The first time, I had underestimated him, and he beat me to a pulp. I survived the eight-second thrashing, but just barely. The second time I had him, I rode much better, even though he had a little weaker day. His weak day was still better than most horses' good days. Now I was faced with the third match-up. I knew that I was in the middle of God's blessings; so did the devil, and the spiritual warfare was on in my mind.

No way can you ride him three times in a row. It's his turn now. As I put my riggin' on Companion, a constant barrage of negative thoughts was beating against my mind like ocean waves on rocks. Companion was definitely healthy, as his wide back stretched out my riggin'. My thought pattern normally as I packed my hand into my riggin' was one of thinking about a strong mark-out and setting my feet, but not that night. There was the onslaught of negative thoughts racing through my head as I was nodding for the gate. However, the last thought through my head was, *I rebuke you, Satan, in the name of Jesus.*

His first three jumps were par for him, as they were real nice. I knew not to get overly aggressive because it wasn't going to stay that nice for the whole eight seconds. And it wasn't long until the jumps got stronger and stronger and stronger. In fact, about the fourth jump was when the power surges started. His circle to the left was started pretty quick and tight. That night was his night to shine.

The farther he went, the higher and harder he dropped out of the air. He would blast my feet back to me, and I'd ram 'em back down as hard as I could.

Somewhere around the five-to-six-second mark in the ride, the whole wide world started dropping out from underneath me. His front end would rip from the sky as he'd kick over his head. With the G-forces wrenching on my face and body, I'd drive my feet back down and get

DALE HIRSCHMAN

a hold of his big front end. Each jump I survived, but I didn't know if I would the next one. Then the whistle blew. As I dropped my feet to the horse's belly, I reached down to double-grab. In that split second of my body losing momentum and becoming dead weight, ol' Companion jerked the riggin' out of my riding hand, sending me to the terra firma. That was the third time that I'd been on him, the third time I rode him, and the third time that I didn't make it to the pickup man.

Walking away from the secretaries' trailer, I held a $588 check in my hand. Seventy-five dollars went to Marty, leaving just a hair over five hundred dollars for tithes and a trip to Cheyenne, Wyoming. Along with that check, I held a deeper revelation of our heavenly Father's love and faithfulness.

Psalm 37:4 is not a scripture that we use to try and manipulate God into giving us whatever we want, as some might think. Besides, we must fulfill the condition before we receive the promise. And the condition of this scripture is to "delight ourselves in the Lord." If we delight ourselves in Him, then our motives won't be just to reap fleshly desires. Over the years, I've come to believe that the actual meaning of the scripture is, as we delight ourselves in Him, He will *place* His desires in our heart. What better way is there to have pure, godly desires than to have God put them in your heart? I do believe that people will be shocked at how much they enjoy the desires that God gives them. Try Psalm 37:4, and see what God will do.

The Desires of Your Heart
Part Two

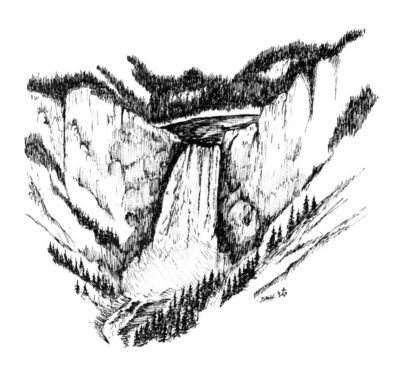

Just when we think we've got God figured out, He does something that throws a kink in our theology. Maybe not always, but often enough that we need to keep an open, teachable mind toward what we believe the Word says—obviously not the foundations of the Word of God, such as Jesus being the Son of God, the virgin birth, Jesus paying for our sins on the cross, and so forth; but we definitely need to keep an open mind on how God works. As the years have swept by since that night in Great Bend, Kansas, as I shared in the previous story, I have come to believe and have preached that the true meaning of Psalm 37:4 is that as we delight ourselves in Him, He will place His desires in us—which I believe with all my heart is true. Philippians 2:13 (NKJV) states, "For it is God who works in you both to will and to do for His good pleasure." However, right in the middle of my die-hard convictions, God rattled my cage.

On a recent family vacation, my family and I went to Yellowstone National Park. For you rodeo cowboys, a vacation is when you go somewhere and you're not entered in a rodeo. I had wanted to go to Yellowstone for as long as I can remember, and I finally made it there. It only took me half a century to get there. I realized that as long as it took me to get there the first time, I didn't know if I would get to go again. So I wanted the trip to be the best possible. With that in mind, my wife went to work researching Yellowstone on the Internet. During the crucial research, she found a cabin in the park with indoor plumbing.

Right close to the top of my desire list was to get to see a grizzly bear. My wife's research on the Internet included searching for information about Yellowstone grizzlies. The slightest chance of seeing grizzlies, according to everything she found, was the month of July. Guess which month was the only month that we were able to go?

DALE HIRSCHMAN

That's right, the month right after June and right before August: July.

With our arrival at Yellowstone, we were greeted with a lot of winding roads, steep drop-offs, breathtaking views, and two buffalo that had traffic stopped bumper to bumper. Except for a little road construction, our introduction to Yellowstone was just what we had expected.

In our research, we jotted down locations where we would see grizzlies, if we were fortunate enough to see any; and we headed to those destinations the first morning of our stay at the park. I had made mention to my heavenly Father several times about my desire to see *Ursus Horribilis,* so I was in high hopes to see one. The winding, shoulderless roads kept our progress from going too fast. Throw in a stop for a herd of elk, and then the viewing of a cow moose and her calf, and our trip to "grizzly land" took us longer than what it looked on the map. But our destination was finally reached.

The area was already covered with quite a few parked cars and people milling around and gazing through spotting scopes. As we got closer, we could see people pointing and looking in one direction. My excitement grew and then really shot up as I realized that my dream was quickly coming true. There was a grizzly down in the valley right next to a fallen tree. And as I squinted and strained to locate the fallen tree, I figured out that I would have to use my 400-meter lens on my camera to see the target of everyone's attention. About three quarters of a mile down in the valley was a dark spot: my grizzly bear. If you looked close, you could make out the basic shape of the grizzly. We watched the spot move around for a while, and then we decided to leave. Walking back to the vehicle, my wife,

Sarah, looked at me and said, "Well, you saw your grizzly." Yes, I did; but I felt short-changed.

Making my way back to our family van was a time spent in prayer. I appreciated the fact that I got to see a grizzly, but I asked my heavenly Father if I could please see one up close. Sitting in the van, I made my declaration, "I was glad to get to see a grizzly. However, I want to see one up close." Instantly, my wife and one of my daughters made their declaration, "Not too close."

That evening, we returned to the grizzly valley, which had several brown dots milling around. One group was a grizzly sow and her two cubs. She had been seen closer to our viewing spot, but she definitely didn't come close that evening. Another group was of a sow and her three cubs. They also never got very close to us. The remaining brown dots were identified by the grizzly bear groupies as lone males. The bears were close enough that, looking through a spotting scope, you could tell their head from their tail; but that was about it. We returned to our cabin for supper with no grizzlies up close yet.

We were not able to go grizzly hunting again until the third day of our trip. My wife and our oldest daughter, Rachel, forsook the ritual of putting on some makeup so that we could leave our cabin thirty minutes before sunrise. We staggered out of the cabin with sleep still in our eyes and piled into our van. The cool darkness of the early morning greeted us as we rambled out of the cabin parking lot. The drive to the location of the grizzly valley, by Mount Washburn, was bad enough in the daylight; but in the dark, it was treacherous for us flat-landers. We arrived there in time to take a few photos of the sun coming up. A few cars had snuck in before us, but not many. They were looking down in the valley as we pulled over. The sow with the two cubs was down at the bottom, closer but still a long ways away. After watching her for a while, we went on down to another viewing spot in hopes of seeing my prayer request manifest with a grizzly coming close.

Just like so many other outdoor activities that deal with wildlife, you hurry up, get there, and wait. And we waited and waited and waited. Two mule deer bucks came up from behind us, but no grizzlies ever came out where we were. A passerby told us that the grizzly sow and her two cubs were coming closer to the road, so we bailed into the van and headed that way. By the grace of God, we found an open spot to park. Before the van was in park, we were unloaded and heading to the side of the road to look down in the valley. We didn't have to look far because about seventy yards off the road was my answered prayer. The sow and her two cubs were making their way up the mountain.

As the trio meandered up the side of the mountain, they stopped and turned over a few rocks to eat whatever was under them. The cubs would wait eagerly while their mother would turn over the rock. Then they'd dive in and lick up whatever came scurrying out. I learned later that the grizzlies in Yellowstone often associate people with roads, so they do not think much of the human spectators and go about their everyday business. It's when they run into a human out on the trails that they might gnaw on you for a while. With us being road huggers, we were ignored by the bears while my youngest daughter and I fired away picture after picture. We enjoyed the show until someone's car alarm went off. Momma grizzly grunted toward us humans and led her cubs off out of sight up the mountain.

Now I had seen grizzlies up close. My heart-felt desire was fulfilled toward the grizzlies. The gift of answered prayer was pretty overwhelming. My heavenly Father blessed me not because He needed to but just because He wanted to. Counting our blessings and being ever so grateful, we made our way back to the Canyon Village area to eat.

I was reflecting over what all had happened in the last two and half days as we hit the road after our noon meal. We had seen every animal that I wanted to see: mule deer in velvet; bull elk; black bear; bull moose; and, of course, the grizzly. Now, as we were heading out again, there was another heart desire not fulfilled: my daughter Rebekah's dream. She shared with me that she wanted to see a wolf and a coyote. We saw several coyotes, and some real close; but that wasn't her true heart's desire. After thanking God for his faithfulness in giving me what I desired, I asked if

DALE HIRSCHMAN

he'd please give Rebekah the desires of her heart and allow her to see a wolf.

The scenario of the wolf sighting was a little different. There were some wolves that were being spotted in one area; however, a couple of wolf watchers came up with the bright idea of sneaking over and ambushing the wolves with their cameras. They did succeed in sneaking up on the wolves, but they also succeeded in driving the wolves back into the mountains. Now, thanks to the thoughtlessness of two individuals, nobody was seeing the wolves at all. Our chance in the wolves reappearing anywhere around us was pretty slim. Plus, we were leaving the next morning. But God had other plans.

We had driven just a few miles when we saw the spotting scopes out and everyone looking in one direction. We pulled over and, through some intense investigation, we found out that an alpha female wolf had come out of the trees. I quickly asked one of the serious wolf-watchers where the wolf was, and he said, "Over there by some trees." I looked in the direction he pointed, and there were the trees, a whole forest of them. So I asked a tourist exactly where the wolf was, and he pointed out which trees the wolf was by. This wolf was so far away that it was a very tiny speck, even through my big camera lenses. Rebekah was not going to see this wolf unless we looked through a spotting scope.

I politely approached a wolf-watcher and asked if my daughter could look through his spotting scope. He growled at us, saying that we could just as long as we "didn't touch his scope." I assured him that we wouldn't, and I helped Rebekah fix her attention on the tan and white wolf way off in the distance. Then I snuck a quick look after Rebekah was done. Rebekah and I walked back to the van, once more overwhelmed by God's goodness. He allowed my daughter to see the wolf she desired to, and not only see it but see it well through the spotting scope. I even got a good look at it.

The following morning, we packed to leave my dream vacation. The things we saw and did were replaying through my mind as I was in a constant state of appreciation to my heavenly Father. One of the events that played again in my mind was when Rebekah and I had gone out by ourselves the second evening. We had just come upon a big bull buffalo close to the road. We pulled over, took several photos of him, and visited with some of the people who were standing around. They mentioned that the buffalo had just swum the river and how impressive it was to watch. That would have been incredible to watch. Once again, I went to who was blessing me so much. I prayed, "Father, I am so content with this trip and thankful for all the blessings you've given me. If you don't mind, may I see a buffalo swim the river before we leave? I thank you, Father, in Jesus's name." We were leaving right at that time; so if God was going to answer that prayer, it was now or never.

We were not on the road more than ten minutes when we rounded a bend in the road and there in Hayden Valley, right by the edge of the Yellowstone River, was not one buffalo but a whole herd of buffalo just starting to enter the river. Once more, there was a parking spot that was open for us right up close to all the action. We bailed out with cameras in hand and went to blasting away with our Nikons. We watched as the entire herd of nearly one hundred head of buffalo swam the Yellowstone. Humbled and grateful, we soaked in every detail of the crossing.

DALE HIRSCHMAN

Once on the other side of the river, I witnessed my unspoken requests as several buffalo went to wallowing and rolling in the dirt. As the buffalo rolled, clouds of dust rose and drifted along the side of the hill. Dust was so thick that the buffalo was barely visible. Then, as if things couldn't get any better, I witnessed another unspoken request come to pass when two buffalo bulls went to fighting on top of the hill. One of the bulls realized that he was in the wrong situation, so he decided to abandon his previous plans of whipping the other bull and leave, but not before I got several photos of the short-lived fight. After watching the answered prayer for thirty-plus minutes, we headed back to the van, again overwhelmed with God's goodness.

Why would God do something like this? Why would He bless me so much? Because He loves me. And He is no respecter of persons. He loves you just as much as He loves me. As we delight ourselves in Him, He will place His desires in us, as I mentioned earlier. But He will also give us our desires that we have in our heart because He loves us. Why? Just because He's our heavenly Father and just because He wants to.

Specific Prayer

A while ago, I heard a story of a hunter who was leaving his deer stand after an unsuccessful day of hunting. During his departure, he unloaded his rifle and put it behind the seat of his pickup, all very typical as well as smart. Before he could drive out of the pasture where he was hunting, a large, eleven-point buck walked out of the brush and stood in the middle of the pasture road, totally and completely still. Now, I know what some of you are thinking, *Of course they stand still when the spotlight hits them.* However, that wasn't the case this time.

The hunter stopped his pickup. The deer stood there. The hunter got out of his pickup. The deer stood there. The hunter got his rifle out from behind the seat of his pickup. The deer stood there. The hunter loaded his rifle. Still, the deer stood there. The hunter put the crosshairs on the deer, and boom, the big boy bit the dust. The hunter loaded the deer in his pickup and headed home. By the time I heard this story, I had spent four or five days in the deer stand, hardly seeing a deer close to being worth shooting. I wished that I'd get a deer on a suicide mission such as the one I had just heard about.

Trying to follow Jesus in my daily life, I decided to pray for God to send me a buck on a suicide mission. The last day of the season, I was back in my deer tower, and

I got a shot at an okay buck. I hit the deer, but he didn't expire right away. He did not go far before he went down. I knew he would die soon, so I waited. As I waited, a four-point buck came out of the woods and started to graze in the wheat field. His antlers were pencil-thin, and he was about as big as a German Shepherd dog—maybe.

As I was waiting, I became impatient. After I had studied the area, I figured that if I could get out of the deer tower, I could sneak around to get another shot at my laying-down buck. However, Mr. Pencil-thin Antlers was in the way. I did not want him to see me for fear that he might spook and cause my buck to jump up and run away also. There was no need to educate that little guy to the fact that hunters hide in the tower in case he was to grow up and someday be a trophy buck himself. After some more thought and consideration, I decided to toss my plastic orange vest out the window, hoping he would see it and retreat back into the woods. Out the window the orange vest flew; and sure enough, he saw it and went back to grazing.

Okay. Now time for plan B. I tied a rope to my backpack and lowered it out of my blind while little bucky was looking the other way. Easing the backpack down until it was in the bushes, I kept close watch on the four-point goofball in the field. I proceeded to raise and lower the bag, making a tremendous racket in the bushes. Knowing that baby bucky would bolt and run to his home in the trees, I watched him closely. Sure enough, he noticed all the commotion in the bushes and went back to eating again.

Plan C was brought to the top of the priority list. The only problem was that there was no plan C. So I

DALE HIRSCHMAN

just climbed down. The adolescent deer never saw me. Once on the ground, I stood there, staring at him. Finally, I spoke. He whirled and gave me that deer-in-the-headlights look. Translated into human language, it would be something like, "Duh."

The little guy took about five or six steps, stopped, and looked at me again. After a few moments, he eased off into the woods. As he disappeared, I realized that God had given me exactly what I had prayed for: a deer on a suicide mission. Next year, I would pray more specific: "Dear God, please send me a *big* deer on a suicide mission."

When you go to a restaurant and the waitress asks you what you want to eat, you don't say, "Oh, just bring me some food." You decide exactly what you want, even how you want it cooked, and you let the waitress know. Why is it that when people pray, we pray something like, "Please bless them/us, God," or, "Please be with them/us"? If you've got a need or a concern, then share it with God. He already knows (Matthew 6:8). It's not like we shock God when we share a concern or even confess a sin to Him. God doesn't go, "I didn't know that about you. Boy howdy, you're in big trouble now, hot shot." God, the One who knows us the best, loves us the most (Romans 5:8). He knows what we have need of before we even ask. He knows when we sin and fall short of His glory. There is no such thing as a secret sin or a secret desire; God knows.

Not only does God know about your needs and your sins, but He is not intimidated by them either. As long as you're alive and kicking, there is not a need or a sin too big for God to meet or forgive. God doesn't see our need and proclaim, "Whoa, baby. That need is too much for Me to handle. I'm sorry. You're on your own." God for sure doesn't sound off, "Gee whiz. You just crossed over the forgiveness line with that sin. This is the last trip to the water fountain for you because it's off to hell now." God is bigger than your biggest sin or need.

Now there are those who will raise the question about the unforgivable sin: blasphemy against the Holy Spirit. I believe that blaspheming the Holy Spirit is when we ignore His wooing in our lives to receive Jesus and His forgiveness before we die. If we sincerely repent for our sins, He will forgive us.

With all this said, we need to pray specifically when we talk to God. We don't surprise, shock, or scare God when we share our deepest needs and failures with Him. Praying specifically helps us realize that it's God meeting our needs when we see the prayer answered. We will realize His faithfulness and His love when we see Him meet the needs that have been presented to Him. Praying specifically will take the coincidence out of the need being met, thus being a witness to others as well as to ourselves. As you draw closer to Jesus in your prayer time, share the intricate desires of your heart with Him. Not only do we deepen our relationship with Him, but we'll see His hand in our lives. By the way, after specific prayer, I shot a big deer the next year!

"Be anxious for nothing, but in everything by prayer and supplication, with thanksgiving, let your requests be made known to God" (Philippians 4:6, NKJV).

My First Deer Season

Trash talking was over, and I was putting actions behind my words. After I turned a quail-hunting invitation into a deer-hunting invitation, I was ready to get started with the deer hunting I'd been talking about doing. Of course, I lacked a few items that I'd need, such as everything that I needed. Horse-trading some artwork for the loan of a deer rifle took care of the most important element on my needs list. The rest of the stuff that I thought I needed I picked up at the ol' Wal-Mart—you know, hunting videos, hunting magazines, doe pee, all that cool stuff us *real* hunters need.

During my childhood days at my grandparents' farm, I learned gun safety and wisdom. The wisdom consisted of such tidbits as: don't point a rifle at another human anytime, don't shoot Grandpa's chickens, and under no circumstances do you ever shoot all the .22 shells your first day on the farm. It might be two or three days before you get to go to town to get more. After all those summers on the farm and the thousands and thousands of .22 shells fired through that old, single-shot rifle, I didn't think that my marksmanship was too far gone from my motor skills. Along with all the childhood practice, I had been "shooting" with my camera, and I believed that kept my marksmanship skills from getting too rusty.

Included in my scavenging for equipment was a hunting partner. My stepdad was a perfect candidate, as we got along great and he had been unable to go hunting the last couple of years. With everything I thought I needed crammed into my cool, hunter-lookin' camouflage bag, a trip to the rifle range, and a secured hunting buddy, I now just needed to go scout the hunting area for deer signs. I

DALE HIRSCHMAN

was also proud of the fact that I was learning more deer-hunting vocabulary all the time.

A trip to my friend GW's ranch and in no time, we were loaded up and headed to the wheat field near the river where I was going to hunt. We were driving around the edge of the wheat field, looking at all the tracks of the calves that GW had in this pasture, when he informed me that he hadn't had any cattle in this pasture for several weeks. Oh my. These were deer tracks, and it looked like cattle tracks in a feedlot. They were everywhere. This was going to be like shooting ducks in a barrel, so I thought.

My stepdad, Bill, arrived at our house the night before the first day of rifle season. There had been some concern as to whether or not Bill was going to be able to go hunting because of a minor surgery that he had that summer. But the doctor said that he was healed up enough from his triple bypass heart surgery to go hunting. We bailed out of bed and were on the road by 4:30 in the morning. A quick stop at a convenient store, which looked like a hunter's orange convention, and then off to GW's place we went. We arrived at 5:30 a.m., ready to get the deer in the crosshairs. After a short conversation with GW, we learned a couple of things: what pickup we were to drive and that GW is not a morning person. He was glad to get back to bed, and we were glad to get on the road again. Crawling into the one-ton, four-wheel-drive farm truck, we should have been suspicious when the steering wheel was mounted upside down; but beggars can't be choosers.

Right away, we knew that if any deer were hiding in the tops of trees, we would see them, as the headlights on dim shone on the tops of the trees. The "brights" never saw any terra firma. Down the road we rolled in style and anticipation as we came to the first of four gates. The key was on the fencepost right by the gate. I forgot to ask what side of the gate and where on the post it was. As the search for the key clicked into the fifteen-minute zone, I decided to call GW. The groggy voice at the other end of the phone told me of another gate that we could go through. After the sheepish thanks from my end of the phone, we were off in hot pursuit of the other gate and the happy hunting grounds, not to be confused with heaven at this point in our lives.

After driving through two more pasture gates without any incidents, we felt more relaxed in the cab of the farm truck. The headlights were irritating in that whenever we went up a slight incline, we would lose sight of the ground; but we were getting closer to our blinds. I had only been in this pasture twice before, and both times were in the daylight, so I was racking my brain trying to remember the road and watch for landmarks.

As we topped a little knoll, the headlights left the earth, and we rolled on in total darkness for a split second. As our lights descended back to earth, everything just disappeared on the left side of the pickup as it slammed into an incline position. Bill smashed into the windshield and slid down the dash onto me as the pickup plummeted at a forty-five-degree angle.

Did I mention that Bill was seventy-two years old and that he just had bypass heart surgery the previous summer? Did I mention that he was laying on me, as we were both shocked and stunned while our world was resting at a sharp angle? I pushed Bill off as he started crawling out his side of the pickup. I squeezed out of my side of the pickup, and we quickly assessed what had happened.

DALE HIRSCHMAN

When I topped the little knoll, I had driven on the edge of a three-foot-deep ravine. The weight of the pickup caved off the side of the ravine, and we went crashing down.

There Bill and I stood, side by side, gazing at the one-ton, four-wheel-drive pickup resting ever so awkwardly in the washout with the right back wheel hovering above the ground.

Bill's voice broke through the silence. "It's stuck. Let's go hunt."

With the thousands of miles that I've driven, I have only had one minor accident. Never had I done something like this with someone else's pickup. There was no way I was going to just walk away. So Bill and I went to work. Besides. It was still dark. We could push this pickup out and still get to the deer stands before daylight.

An hour later, we were still pushing, prying, heaving, and hoeing; and that pickup wasn't going. Finally admitting defeat, I called GW to break the news to him about what I did to his pickup.

"It's stuck. Go hunt," responded GW.

Gee. I'd heard that before. He also told us that if we would cut across the pasture, we'd get to the wheat field, where our deer stands were located, quicker.

The morning light was trying to shine through, but a heavy fog set in and squelched it. The fog was about as close to being a heavy mist as it could be. The ground was soggy with moisture, and the plants painted our legs with a layer of water as we brushed up against them during the trek to our destination. Original plans were to drop our gear off at our blinds, drive the pickup to a hidden spot, and then hike back to the blinds. Had I known that I'd been hiking across country, I'd not "needed" several of the items that had stowed away in my pack. My pack was actually a duffel bag, so it did not fit that well on my back. But hey, it was camouflaged; so it at least looked cool.

Not that far into our cross-country march, we spotted "the" wheat field. We scaled the fence at the best spot located; and across the field we went, as the blinds were on the opposite side of the field. Green wheat and muddy soil created terrain that definitely lacked traction. It was step and slide, step and slide as we slogged along. Sometimes, our feet would step and slide forward; and other times, we'd step and slide backward. More than we wanted, one foot would slide back and the other would slide forward at the same time. We weren't seeing any of the landmarks that I had picked out earlier, but we trudged on and kept looking.

About fifty yards into the field we spotted a truck parked off to the side and someone was in it. Now this really irritated me because GW told me that no one else would be hunting on his land. Why do people do things like hunt on someone else's property without permission? I felt like going over and asking him what he was doing, but the walking was tough enough without going that far out of my way. Besides, my pack wasn't getting any lighter. As we continued on, I noticed that the pickup started moving and coming toward us. Good. It looked like I would get my chance to ask this guy what he was doing on someone else's property without permission.

With the fact that I hadn't noticed any of my landmarks haunting my mind, I started getting this sinking feeling as the pickup drew closer. The sinking feeling started to turn to nausea as the pickup pulled to a stop in front of us.

"What are you all doing?" came from the truck.

Duh. What does it look like? ran through my mind. However, that pit in my stomach wouldn't let me say that. I was admitting my mistake at the same time as my question came out of my mouth.

"This isn't GW's land, is it?"

"Nope. It's mine."

"Which direction is GW's land?"

"West of here."

My gut feeling, the one that had been correct lately, told me GW's land was to the east. However, I did not argue with a landowner when I was on his land and he was heavily armed!

Westward we went. Too bad that guy couldn't offer a friendly ride to a couple of bewildered gentleman with awkward, overloaded packs. I thought, *Don't you worry about us, Bubba. We'll make it.*

Finally, out of the wheat field we marched, along through the pasture to the "west." The ground had a lot more traction now, as we plowed through the underbrush and thistles, over hill after hill, drifting back and forth to see if we could see a wheat field as we topped each knoll. There was still a misty haze saturating the atmosphere. Even though all my clothes were waterproof, I was soaked from the inside out. There was not a dry fiber anywhere on my boots, and they were stretching.

Now my step-slide was inside my boots. My legs were heavy, my pack was heavy, my breathing was heavy, and I hadn't gone through triple-bypass heart surgery. Bill was still going, so I guess the doctor was right. He was healed enough to go hunting. But I bet when the ol' doctor said that, he didn't know that hunting involved getting thrown into a windshield, pushing and shoving on a stuck pickup, and then hiking all over the countryside. My ego took another hit as I told Bill that I thought we'd better head back to the pickup.

Over two hours after we left the pickup, we arrived back at the peculiarly parked pickup, and we sat down. Now that felt good. I mean it felt *good*. One item that I had in my oversized, over-packed backpack was a first-aid

DALE HIRSCHMAN

kit, which now came in very handy as I peeled my socks off. The blisters on my feet welcomed the Band-Aids. If my feet could smile, I'm sure they were then--at least until I put the wet boots back on. The last tug and lacing up on the boots was met with GW pulling up with towrope in hand. Several laughs—few of them were mine—and tugs later, the pickup was out of the ravine, and we were loaded in GW's pickup, headed to the deer blinds. Being that it was now after 10:30 a.m., the morning deer rush hour at the wheat field was more than likely over. However, with the heavy fog just now achieving lift-off, we were hoping for some late arrivals at the food plot. Since GW knew where we were going, we were dropped off at our deer blinds in no time at all.

Establishing my home away from home in the blind was next on my agenda. Snags in my game plan just kept creeping up. Now my campstool that was tied to my backpack was gone. There was absolutely no way I was going to backtrack to see if I could find it. I considered that baby a contribution to the great outdoors. After realizing that I couldn't see over the top of my blind if I just sat on the ground, I stood up and volunteered my backpack as my new campstool.

No sooner than right after I got it situated, a *splat* hit my backpack. Then another *splat* and another and another and then bunches of them as the rain came. *Ha. I'm ready for you, Mr. Rain. I've got my Wal-Mart rain poncho in my overstuffed backpack.* Slipping it on, I sat down and puffed up like a big ol' toad under a waterspout. And I stayed puffed up for the next three hours as it rained and rained and rained.

With nothing moving all morning and early afternoon except me wiggling under my poncho, I decided to head back to the pickup. Several times, I had wondered how Bill was doing because he had been out of sight most of the morning. I would drive the pickup down to his blind to pick him up as soon as I was at the hidden parking spot. However, I learned how Bill was doing, as he was sleeping in the pickup when I arrived. Waking him up, we loaded up and headed out. Next year, we might even see a deer.

In the first chapter of the book of James, verses 2–4 encourage us to, "... count it all joy when you fall into various trials, knowing that the testing of your faith produces patience. But let patience have its perfect work, that you may be perfect and complete, lacking nothing" (NKJV).

DALE HIRSCHMAN

Looking back at that "hunt" I noticed the attitude that Bill displayed as I led him on a wild goose chase searching for deer. Never once did he gripe or become angry as we faced constant setback and trial at each turn of our adventure. The hunt did not turn out anything like what we had imagined it would or desired for it to, but Bill took it all in stride and made the most of a bad situation.

Maybe, just maybe, if we all will learn to take more of life's happenings in stride and not get worked up when things don't go as we planned, then we will become perfect (literally means "mature"), lacking nothing. Who knows? The next time we go through obstacles and maintain good attitudes, we might see the deer we're after or whatever we're pursuing!

Deer Surfing

Each year of my deer-hunting career, my good friend, GW Harrel, has let me hunt on his land. This year was no exception. The first weekend of the rifle season found my stepfather, Bill McLean, and me in our usual blinds. Our enthusiasm was met with rain, warm weather, and no deer movement. Thus, our first weekend hunting left us with no deer; but we still had two weeks left in the hunting season.

The last weekend had arrived, and I still had two unfilled deer tags. A special doe season was scheduled for December, so I wasn't too worried about fillin' the doe tag. However, an unfilled buck tag was creating some anxiety! With a basketball tournament eating up my Saturday, my last chance to hunt was after church on Sunday. And, it was raining! I would not complain about rain in western Oklahoma, and I was thankful for all the rain we had gotten that year, but a break in the rain would have been nice.

Then the rain stopped, and I was off to Leedey. My buck tag was soon to be filled—I hoped. It wouldn't have been so bad that I hadn't seen any bucks except for the fact that almost everyone else had. To be exact, all of GW's grandkids, except for one, had shot a buck. I hadn't even seen anything in the deer family.

I arrived at GW's place, and I headed straight to the deer stand, which was located by the Canadian River. As I pulled up to the ranch gate, I was met by my friend, Charles, and his crew—CJ, Brandon, Josh, and Jacob. They were all in camouflage, and they were carrying the news of CJ's seven point buck. The pressure to get a buck intensified with the bringing of the news. I was headed to the deer stand with the determination not to be out-hunted by a bunch of six- to twelve-year-old kids!

Even though there was a lot of rain, most of the ground was river sand and pretty easy traveling. Places where things were on the boggy side, I made up for not having four-wheel-drive with my pickup's speed.

After a quick drive, gates that I never could get open quick enough, and a walk to the deer stand, I was finally in the deer stand. The time was 4:00 in the afternoon, and I was settled in. I scanned the trees along the edge of the wheat field, watching for any movement. Nothing seemed to be moving except a squirrel and some birds. I could not believe that I hadn't seen anything yet. I wondered what time it was. So I dug through my clothes to find my watch. It was 4:10. Okay. Now I relaxed and waited.

By 4:20, I saw movement in the trees, and a doe stepped out. After the doe stepped out, I saw the rear end of a deer stepping through all the brush; and this one was walking like John Wayne. For some reason, I knew that this one was a buck by the walk. Besides, no self-respecting girl would want to walk like John Wayne, even in the deer family. As the buck strolled into view, I could tell he was just a six-point buck. But he was a buck, and he was of decent size. I made the executive decision to take the shot if he gave me any chance. He was just a few steps

DALE HIRSCHMAN

from being in the open when he stopped, looked over his shoulder, and then turned and started walking back into the trees.

The sound of my jaw hitting my chest didn't spook anything as I watched in astonishment as my deer walked away. Now my only chance to shoot this guy was if he would walk through about a four-foot opening that I had noticed earlier. He was heading straight toward it. I aimed at the elbow, squeezed the trigger, and the rifle recoiled with the sound of the shot. In that split second, I saw the deer jump and run with a stiff-legged stride. He only went about fifteen feet when he stopped and lay down. After watching my share and someone else's share of hunting shows, I had the urge to holler, "Big buck down." However, my conscience wouldn't let me yell something like that for just a six-point buck; so, I whispered, "Medium buck down."

The time was 4:40 in the evening, so I kicked back to give the deer time to expire. You know us "experienced hunters" know not to rush down to where the animal went down for the likelihood that a person might startle the wounded animal, and it would disappear to be never found by a human again. Being in the self-confident mood for bein' such a fine shot and all, I was looking forward to getting to tell everyone (especially those under ten years old) that I finally got a buck.

Curiosity was on the upswing as to why my deer hadn't expired yet after lying there for forty-five minutes. But I knew he was just seconds away from going to the wheat field in the sky. As I started gathering my gear (you know, the important deer hunting equipment: my water bottle, sunflower seeds, Hot Tamales candy—all the necessities for deer hunting), I noticed something different. My deer got up and walked away! I could not believe it. I knew that I hit him when I shot. I could tell by the way he reacted when I fired. And now he just got up and walked away!

After climbing down from the tree stand, I eased over to see if I could find any blood trails, but it was now too dark to see. As I made my way back toward the tree stand, I could hear something breaking its way through the brush in the river bottom where I was. Figuring it was my ex-buck, I exited as quietly as I could. *Tomorrow after school, I'll make a run back up here to see if I can find my needle-in-a-haystack buck.* Diving into my old clothes as soon after school as I could, my green Dodge Dakota and I took off to Leedey again. I drove as close as I could to the deer stand, which meant crossing a small creek along the way. Even though the creek was up from all the rain, my little Dodge blew right through, slinging mud and water everywhere. On to my destination, the edge of the wheat field by the river bottom we went. Five o'clock had already arrived by the time I started my search, so I was running out of time. *Over the fence and through the woods to deer carcass I go.*

The whole area was a marsh with all the precipitation that we had. My knee-high rubber boots and I tromped and splashed to the spot where I last saw the deer. From that point, I searched to the east, where I had heard the ruckus the night before. The more I trudged eastward, the deeper the water level became. Now, I'm not a rocket scientist; but you don't have to be one to figure out that a wounded deer wouldn't head into deeper water to find a place to get off his feet. I returned to the original starting point and headed uphill. Low and behold, about seventy-five yards through the brush, log piles, and marshy conditions was a little patch of white and tan underneath a tree. My deer had finally expired, and more important than that, I found him.

I heaved him out from underneath the tree and determined right away that I was not going to drag him through everything without making him as light as possible, which meant field-dressing him. I'd never field-dressed a deer before; but I'd seen it done twice. So, with full confidence I went to work. My deer had been dead now for twenty-four hours, plus he was gut shot. My bullet placement was off a little—well, maybe a fair amount—more than what I want to admit. As my skinning knife sliced through the skin, I was met with a *pssst* sound from the deer. I'm not a stranger to passing gas, but this had to be one of the rankest yet. I sliced and cut, gasped and grabbed, lifted and shook, pinched and pulled until finally the entrails all came out.

Sweat was running off my forehead and dripping to the beat of the howling coyotes all around me, and now I was ready for the real work. It was time to drag this rascal out of there. I looped my rope around the neck of this 125-pound, field-dressed deer and began to drag. I felt like things were going good and that I was clipping along at a good pace when I was yanked to a screeching halt. His antlers were tangled in some brush about ten feet from where we had started. Maybe I wasn't going as fast as I thought. Jerking his head out of the brush, I tugged along some more.

This time, as I started, I believe he weighed somewhere around 135 to 140 pounds. Ducking down under low-hanging limbs, dragging him over fallen logs, I was sure he weighed around 185 pounds. At another fifty yards with the sweat dripping off my face, my legs starting to weaken, he was weighing around 265 pounds. Thirty more yards over more fallen lumber and across the small creek at the edge of the wheat field and I got my 315-pound buck about six feet from the fence. A four-foot-high incline creek bank was my last obstacle. No problem though. I was fixin' to drag that baby outta there with my pickup.

My Jell-O legs and I loped to the pickup where I eased the ol' Dodge into position. Bailing out, I quickly tied the rope to the bumper of my pickup. With a pickup on one end of the fifty-foot rope, a deer on the other end, and forty feet of slack in between the two, I started to drive off. One slight problem arose. My tires were spinning, but my pickup wasn't going anywhere. The downhill side of that wet, muddy wheat field just wasn't providing the traction my pickup needed. No problem. My Dodge Dakota and I started doing the rocking motion: forward, reverse; forward, reverse. The pickup finally started moving but was bouncin' and slingin' mud as we went. The RPM's showed that we ought to be going a lot faster than what we were, but we were moving; and I guarantee you I was not stopping.

About that time, all the slack was jerked out of the rope and ol' bucky was jerked up over the creek bank by the rope tied to his hind feet. I kept givin 'er the gas, the pickup was bouncin' and flingin,' and that deceased deer was skiing along behind in the wake. High ground was the destination, and we finally made it. I shut it down and went back and drug Bambi's cousin the last forty feet.

DALE HIRSCHMAN

With him loaded in the bed of the pickup, I headed toward the wheat field's gate. Stopping at the gate, I got out to open it. I shot a glance back at my deer. Talk about shrinkage! He was back down to 125 pounds!

In Matthew 7:3(NKJV), it states, "And why do you look at the speck in your brother's eye, but do not consider the plank in your own eye?" This verse is dealing with, among other issues, the perspective we use when we look at different things. The closer we are to something, the bigger it looks to us.

When I was draggin' that deer over logs and through all the underbrush, he sure did look a lot bigger than he was. But, when he was loaded in the pickup and all the work was done, he really didn't look that big!

When we are smack dab in the middle of tough circumstances, our perspective on how things look can really become distorted. If we make decisions in the midst of that distortion, those decisions can often be the wrong ones. We've got to learn to back up and look at our circumstances from a distance so we can get the proper perspective! I've heard people talk about backing up and looking at things as learning to look at things from God's perspective, from the way He sees things; knowing that He sees the whole picture and not just the small part that we see. He sees the beginning and the end; we just see where we are in that present moment of time. I believe, as we learn to back up and look at things, we'll see a lot more shrinkage in our problems.

Deer Hunting: Big Boy

After the horrendous bullet placement on my buck from the previous season, my confidence in shooting had taken a pretty hard hit. A couple of trips to the rifle range with my new rifle and a box of shells fired and my confidence was restored some. The new hunting backpack was loaded, more bullets were purchased, deer tags were bought, hunting clothes were washed and dry, and we were ready to go.

The first day of rifle season found us—my stepdad, Bill, and me—heading back to GW's place down by the river. Bill only had one day that he could hunt, so he got top priority on the deer that came by. He was in a pop-up blind that I had, and I was in the tower an hour before the sun rose above the horizon line. After half of the day was gone, we really didn't have much chance of shooting anything, but the afternoon was different. Bill got a shot at a young buck that he hit, but the buck ran into the river. We had to track him later. As we were waiting for the buck's expiration date to arrive, a doe walked out into the field. I figured that I'd shoot this one since Bill shot the last one. Just as I was raising my rifle, *Boom!* Bill shot that one too.

The doe was hit solid, but was still headed to the river. I had a better angle to finish off the doe than Bill, so I took aim and shot. And I missed, which was okay because I hurried. I chambered another round, took better aim, and missed again. The third shell was chambered, aimed better than the last shot, and I missed again. The doe eased over into the river, the last place I wanted her to be. I could not believe that I missed her three times. I was repulsed that I had missed so many times.

Arriving back at GW's, we shared our story. GW listened to our Wild West tale, and then told me, "You're doing something wrong when you shoot." My scope wasn't set perfect, but it wasn't so far off that I should miss when I shot. GW told me that before I came out the next day to stop by the shale pit and to dry-fire my rifle. Dry firing a rifle is shooting the rifle with an empty chamber. I was to pay special attention to what happened to my crosshairs when I pulled the trigger.

Right after church, I headed to the shale pit with three boxes of freshly purchased shells, along with the rest of my hunting gear. I found the shale pit just as easy as GW

DALE HIRSCHMAN

said I would. After stepping off fifty yards, I set up my rifle rest and commenced the dry-firing. Wow. My education started quickly. The first time, I flinched even before I pulled the trigger. Studying the crosshairs as I pulled the trigger, I realized that I was shoving the rifle with my left hand to compensate for the recoil of the rifle. The crosshairs jumped six inches to the right at fifty yards. That's twelve inches or more at one hundred yards. A lot of deer can be missed by that much rifle movement.

After dry-firing several more times, I fired some live rounds through the new rifle. I realized that my scope was off four inches in the same direction that I was moving my rifle each time I shot. Sixteen inches of movement at one hundred yards will miss every deer. I readjusted my scope and continued to dry-fire and fire live rounds. Each time I shot, I had to readjust the paper target. I was trying as hard as I could to shoot correctly and get everything perfect. Two inches high at fifty yards makes yada, yada, yada. I was straining, my crosshairs were jumping, and the fifty-yard dashes were taking up too much time.

Finally, as I was repositioning the target, I noticed some dirt clods about the size of a softball laid all around. I went back to my chair and took aim at the dirt clods. *Boom!* I hit high and to the right just like I used to shoot when I was a kid. Flashback to childhood days. Aim a little low and to the left. *Boom!* and the dirt clod went to rock heaven. Pretty soon, other dirt clods started going to rock heaven, and I was having fun again. I laid three dirt clods in a row and then chambered and fired three shots as fast as I could. All three dirt clods disintegrated before my eyes. *Watch out,* Mr. Buck. *I'm back.*

GW had already told me that I would have to hunt a different spot because of us shooting up the tower area the day before. According to his wisdom, the deer wouldn't dare stick their heads out. As he took me to another blind, he told me how some others tried to hunt the tower area that morning and did not see a single deer. "I wish they would have listened to me," GW told me as we entered into the wheat field where I would be hunting. There was another tower in this wheat field as well as a ground blind. As we drove past the tower, GW told me that I could hunt from it if I wanted, but he thought the best place to hunt from was the ground blind.

In no time, I was dropped off at the ground blind and getting situated. Scoping out the field in front of me, I noticed it was a long way to the edges of the wheat field from where the blind was. I'd never shot at anything that far away, so I figured that I'd just let them come out into the wheat field farther. The ground blind was plenty big enough, and the windows were lined up so that the deer couldn't see my silhouette.

One of the last things that GW told me was that the place had not been hunted, so I might see deer, and I might not see any deer. I was dropped off at 3:00 p.m. At 3:30, I saw two little does walking through on the far side of the wheat field, and that was it. At the other place, we saw deer moving all day long; and here almost nothing.

The tower back west of me was looking more appealing all the time. I decided to go hunt from the tower! Grabbing most of my gear, I snuck out of the ground blind and stalked my way over to the tower. Peeking around to see if I could spot any deer spying on me, I slithered up the ladder and into the tower. Everything looked good

DALE HIRSCHMAN

from up there. I spotted one deer trail and a ravine that deer could be coming up to get to the wheat field, plus I could see ninety percent of the wheat field where I was earlier. I was feeling pretty comfortable with my decision to move when I remembered what GW had said about some other hunters not listening to him. And he did say that he thought that it would be best to hunt out of the ground blind.

First Samuel 15:22 (NKJV) says, "… to obey is better than sacrifice," and multiple other times throughout the Bible, God talks to us about being obedient. The first verse of Romans 13 (NKJV) tells us, to "be subject to the governing authorities." GW was definitely the governing authority over his land, and he knew far more than I did about hunting. Come to think of it, GW did tell me he thought it would be best if I hunted from the ground blind!

At fifteen minutes until five o'clock, a person should really not be moving around; but I was not going to stay in the tower another minute. I gathered my stuff, and trying my best to look invisible, I descended the ladder. Off through the brush I went. Peeking out of the sagebrush, I stole my way across the last opening and into the ground blind to stay.

Forty minutes later and nothing had moved other than me in the blind; and hopefully, I wasn't seen. It was 5:30 p.m., sunset; and I was tempted to leave. The only deer that I had seen were the two little does around 3:30 p.m., and that was it. After some consideration, I decided to stay until it was pitch black outside. No sooner than after my executive decision to stay, a small, three-point buck came out into the wheat field. He took off after two does that had slipped into the field without my noticing them.

While keeping an eye on the little, three-point goofball chasing the does away, I glanced around the field and spotted a spike buck wandering out of the trees. In just ten minutes, the wheat field went from being barren to a bustling deer playground.

The three-point, hormone-charged buck reminded me so much of a high school freshman that I almost shot him but I refrained. Just as I decided to spare his life, he started walking straight toward the ground blind. He was on a crash course, heading straight toward me. About thirty yards from me, he hesitated and looked toward Mr. Spike Buck. My glance went toward ol' spikey in time to see him jerk his head up and stare back into the woods. Deer will see each other long before we see them usually, and this was no exception as a doe trotted into the field.

A few strides behind her swaggered the biggest buck I had ever seen. The evening light danced off his antlers that looked to be two feet above his head. (I know they weren't, but they sure did look like it.) He strolled around with a walk that showed he knew he was the head honcho of this wheat field.

DALE HIRSCHMAN

I've watched tons of hunting shows, and I've always kind of laughed to myself whenever a big buck would walk out and the hunter would start huffing and puffing, trying to breathe. Well, guess who went to huffing and puffing when ol' big boy stepped out. *This is a monster buck,* I thought. Now I know that there are a lot of deer larger than what I was looking at, but none of them were in this field. And with my frame of reference at this point in time, he was a monster buck.

I was in the field that day to shoot a big doe and not a buck, unless he was really big. This guy fit into the "really big" category. As I kept my eyes on the big buck, I reached for my rifle that was leaning up against the side of the blind. Drumming the rifle barrel on the side of the blind reminded me of the little, three-point hooligan buck just thirty yards away from me.

His eyes were riveted on the blind as I froze. The evening sun was low enough, plus the blind was dark enough that I figured he couldn't see me. He slowly diverted his attention back to the big guy in the corner of the field. I was relieved to see him head that direction. I was really glad he wasn't a doe because if he would have been a doe, he would have found a reason to spook at my noise level in the ground blind. Letting the little buck put some distance between him and me, I eased my rifle out the window and put the crosshairs on the big boy. He was a long way away from me, so I didn't even try to make the shot. Besides, I just knew that the doe would lead him further out into the field. Sure enough, she didn't. The doe turned around and walked back into the trees. The buck with the biggest antlers I'd ever seen did an about-face and started to follow her. I thought to myself, *If you turn one more time and give me a broadside shot, I will take it.* Right after I thought that, the buck heard a noise to his right and turned to look. There was my broadside shot. This was by far the longest shot I'd ever tried to make.

I aimed at his shoulder and about halfway down his side. Then the shale-pit practice from earlier that day came to memory. A little low and to the left now became my aim as I dropped off the deer's shoulder along his side just a little. I left the crosshairs on the middle of his side because of the distance. The crosshairs were as steady as a rock as I slowly squeezed the trigger. The time span from the start of the squeeze until the blast and recoil of the rifle seemed like an eternity.

Now everything went into high gear as I chambered another round while I tried to locate him through my scope. When I located him again, he was running backward, dragging his front right leg; so I knew that I had hit him solid in the shoulder. One thing that GW had told me was that if you shoot a big deer and he doesn't drop in his tracks, put another one in him. So, I did. The big guy hit the turf, but he tried to get up again, and I did not want him getting into the trees. I put the final round in him, and he went down to stay.

There was no way I could stay in the blind for thirty minutes to make sure he had expired and no way was I going to go check on him before the thirty minutes was up. In my adrenaline fit, I reached a compromise. I headed back to GW's to get help. Plus, if he really was as big as I thought he was, I wanted someone there to share the discovery of what I shot.

The drive to GW's took way too long. I was tickled that both GW and his wife, Karen, came with me to pick

DALE HIRSCHMAN

up the prize in the wheat field. Along the way back, we were joined by their hired hand, Robert. Arriving back at the wheat field, we drove straight across it to where I thought the deer was. We found him about twenty feet away from where I had shot him. As the headlights shone on the deceased deer, we could see that he rolled over on his back and stuck his antlers into the ground. I thought, *If he broke one of his antlers while he was rolling around in the grass, I'll kill him*… Oh, wait, I already had! My second thought was, *What if he really wasn't very big?* So I asked GW when he saw the deer, regardless of its size, to holler, "Man, Dale. That's a big deer." I was relieved to see that there wasn't that much shrinkage from what I thought he looked like earlier, and GW humored me by hollering, "Man, Dale. That's a big deer." That night, I checked in a ten-point buck that weighed in field-dressed at 150 pounds even.

Replaying the hunt over and over in my mind, I realized how much God had blessed me with the whole ordeal. I also thought about the role that GW played in the hunt. First, he let me hunt on his land. Second, if I'd not practiced the way GW had told me, then I'd never have known that my scope was off and the mistakes I was making while firing. I also realized that the big boy came out in the wheat field in the 10 percent of the field that I could not see from the tower; so if I'd stayed in the tower instead of hunting from the ground blind like GW told me to, then I would have never even seen the buck that is now hanging on my wall. That time, if I hadn't obeyed, I would have sacrificed a big buck! So, next year if GW tells me he thinks I would do better hunting deer by throwing rocks from a fifty-five-gallon barrel, then I'll find some rocks and a fifty-five-gallon barrel!

DALE HIRSCHMAN

Big Boy Two

After being blessed by getting to shoot a really nice trophy buck in 2005, I was told several times that I should not expect to shoot another buck close to that size. I don't like to go after something with low expectations, no matter what it is. When I rodeoed, I expected to win, especially in the later years as I became more serious about it. When I go buy something, I expect to get a good deal. When I go to church, I expect to receive from God; so why should I expect any less when I go hunting? The Bible, in Proverbs 12:2 (NIV), says, "A good man obtains favor from the Lord"; so I expect good things to happen in my life, and they do.

After going out twice during black-powder season and not seeing anything, I went out the first day of rifle season. GW put me in a good blind, but just like the two previous hunts, I didn't see anything. During the midday, I went over to GW's to visit with him and thaw out a little. From there, we went over to deer camp, where several other hunters were staying. We had a brief excursion, and then we settled into deer camp for the social aspects of deer hunting. We looked over a couple of nice deer that were taken earlier that morning. One of them was taken by Brandon, GW's grandson. This was a typical occurrence, as Brandon was an accomplished hunter at the ripe old age of eight. During the multitude of conversations, one individual told me when he used to hunt he would pour doe urine all over the bottoms of his boots before he walked to his blind. The bucks would smell it and often follow his trail right to the blind where he was. I love to teach and I love to learn, so that was some info I stored away.

Break was over, and the time to return to the blinds had arrived. Robert took me to the blind behind GW's house. There had been several large deer shot from that spot, so I was excited to get to hunt out of that blind. I was sitting in the blind, watching Robert walk away, when I remembered, *The doe pee. I didn't use the doe pee.* While Robert was still in sight, I jumped out of the blind, jerked out my bottle of doe pee, and started splashing it all over the bottom of my boots. I jogged up and down the trail

DALE HIRSCHMAN

that I traversed just moments earlier. Then I slung some around in front of my blind. I felt relieved as I finished with the doc pee.

The time was around two o'clock when I settled into my blind. The next three hours went without incident, other than a bobcat that snuck by in the bushes. I had been watching to the north and east, as that was where the deer would be coming from as they made their way to the wheat field west of me. For some reason unbeknownst to me, I looked over my shoulder to the southwest; and there, about twenty feet away from my deer blind, came a small, eight-point buck with his nose to the ground. He was hot on the trail of a doe that had been peeing all over the place. Little did he know that it was me who poured it out of a bottle. The only part of me that moved was my arm as I reached down and opened that good ol' bottle of doe urine to help cover my scent. I was pleasantly surprised that he never did detect me, as I had the privilege to watch him for several minutes. Finally, he eased off out of sight into the bushes, and I was by myself, enjoying God's creation again.

I normally hunt alongside a wheat field, so I wasn't used to how dark the creek area got as the sun went down. The sky was still light, but the shadows were getting hard to see into as the day drifted into late evening. The crack of a branch made my head snap around toward the sound. There, sneaking by in the shadows, was the form of a deer. I brought my binoculars up in a heartbeat and tried to zero in on the passing deer. What is hard to see with the naked eye is often easier to see through binoculars. And whoa, what I saw. I barely had him in the view-finder when I knew that he was a buck. A quick glance directed toward his head gear showed that he was blessed with a nice hat rack.

What really impressed me was that this guy looked more like a bull instead of a deer. He had a neck on him that would not quit. It looked like it grew straight out from behind his ears before it started toward his back. His thick neck was attached to thick shoulders and a flourishing body. He was a very well-rounded individual.

My decision to harvest this big boy was a no-brainer for me. He paused to eat right smack dab in the middle of one of my shooting lanes—his mistake. Barely being able to see his form with the naked eye, I quickly raised my rifle to look through the scope. As I brought the rifle up, I exhaled to calm down for the shot; but as I looked through the scope, all I could see was gray.

What was wrong with my scope? I pointed my rifle up to the sky to get more light through it. I could see somewhat better; and then I realized that as I raised my rifle and exhaled, I fogged up my scope. Now that was a great

DALE HIRSCHMAN

move. I heard another snap of a branch, and I thought, *Oh no. He moved.* I glanced around and couldn't see where he moved to. Panic almost set in until I looked back where he was, and he hadn't moved. I quickly raised my rifle and exhaled as I started to peer through the scope. I did it again. I fogged up my scope again when I exhaled!

I was feeling just like I was related to Barney Fife. I quickly looked through my binoculars. He was still there, but now he was looking back at me. I knew that my time was extremely short at getting a chance to shoot him. This time, I pointed my rifle at him while holding my head beside it. I eased my head sideways and looked through my scope. Wow. I could see clearly now that the gray cloud was gone. I stuck the crosshairs right behind his shoulder, as he was quartered away from me, and I pulled the trigger. The fire jumped out of the barrel and lit up the evening as I tried to keep sight through the recoil.

My last view of the deer was of him coming back down from a jump. His white tail flashed as he disappeared out of sight. Now my ears went to work as I listened for him running away. I heard him run for a second, and then all went quiet. Suddenly, I heard branches break and the noise of a deer crashing through the timber and running off up the creek. A big, sick, ugly feeling rose up in me. I really, really hoped that wasn't my deer that ran off.

I sat there in my blind and gathered up my stuff as slow as I could. I knew I was going to have to wait a while before I went to look for the big boy. I have absolutely no idea how people can sit in a blind for thirty minutes to an hour after they have shot a big deer. I packed up and fidgeted for an eternity of about ten minutes, and I thought I'd sneak out of the blind and go get the pickup. It was dark by now; and besides, if that was my deer that ran off down the creek, he was so far away by now that he'd never see me anyway. I slipped out, got the pickup, and drove back down as far as I could. After thinking things over, I decided getting help from someone would be probably the best way to retrieve the deer. Just as I started back up the hill, I saw the flashlight of help on the way. Charles and his son, Christopher, had noticed that my pickup was gone and came to help.

I located my landmark from where I had shot the deer, and we started our search up the hill in the direction that I had originally seen the deer go. The sounds of a deer running off down the creek still haunted me as we started our search. We made our way up the creek in search of Mr. Big Boy. We were looking for a blood trail as we went.

Even if Charles would have been a world-renowned singer, his voice would not have sounded any better than it did when I heard him say, "Here he is." I almost hurt myself getting around the tree that was between Charles and me.

That fat deer was so nice to see lying there in the tall grass about thirty yards away from where he had been shot. His body was almost totally round from his neck back to his rear. There was very little dip-in for the shoulders and the hip. His neck was as thick as it could be. This was by far the biggest-bodied deer that I'd ever shot! As I "forced" myself to look at his headgear (there is some sarcasm in that last statement), I noticed that he had a long spike growing out of the base of his left antler. He was a nice, wide, unusual eight-point conversation piece; and we found him.

DALE HIRSCHMAN

As I think back, I am so amazed at the favor and blessings that our heavenly Father bestows upon us! This was my sixth year of deer hunting; and I've shot two nice bucks, deer that a lot of deer hunters never get a chance to even see, let alone shoot. God is so good, and He will bless us if we will trust Him and follow after Him. Thank You, Jesus. And thank you, GW and Charles for allowing me to hunt and for helping me so much. "For the Lord God is a sun and shield; the Lord will give grace and glory; no good thing will He withhold from those who walk uprightly!" (Psalm 84:11, NKJV).

One More Story

My oldest daughter was in the infant stage of life and seemed to change every day as she grew older. When I left for a college rodeo and came home from the trip, she had always grown and changed while I was away. The idea of me leaving for several days wasn't even a consideration to me, so that might be why the Holy Spirit started working on my wife, Sarah, first. More than likely, it was also because women tend to be more sensitive to the wooing of the Spirit than men; but that's harder for us men to admit. Either way, the Holy Spirit started working on Sarah's heart about me going to the College National Finals Rodeo. She encouraged me to pray about going; but I have to admit, I really wasn't interested in going at that time because of the previously mentioned reasons. After praying and thinking about the trip to the CNFR, Sarah and I were in agreement that I should head north to the college finals in Bozeman, Montana.

During this time in our lives, we were holding a Bible study for the college students; and there was a good group of students coming, of which several were qualified for the finals. I had the privilege to get to not only watch them compete, but arrangements were made so that I would stay with two of them while I was in Bozeman. In conjunction with the finals, the NIRA was holding a bucking horse and bull sale. I could compete in it as well as support those near and dear to our hearts. Even though I would be away from my family, I was starting to get excited about going. (I even scheduled a rodeo to enter along the way to my destination.)

A few years had passed since I was in Bozeman, so I discovered quite a few changes in the cityscape; but there were a few things that were still the same: the atmosphere of athletic competition for the ultimate goal in college rodeo and the local late-night hangout, The Cat's Paw. The latter came into play as the Finals rolled along.

Our Bible study members were hanging extremely tough throughout the go-rounds of competition, with several of them in line to qualify for the short-go the last day of the rodeo.

One of our Bible study members was trying to get together with some of his friends from out of state so they could get caught up on old times and the *only* place that seemed logical to congregate at was the Cat's Paw. Now, I was not there; so I can only speculate what actually happened. But the following is what I gathered from those involved in one way or another. Our Bible study member, who we'll call Jeff, took another member of the Bible study crew, who we'll call Jimmy, with him to the Cat's Paw. They arrived early, hoping the others would arrive early and they could go somewhere else or at least leave before the place got rough and rowdy. The first hitch in their get-along happened when they got there early and the other party did not. No real problem. They would just shoot pool until the others arrived.

We are still in the speculation zone; but if you think about it, there's just so many "cokes" that you can drink

DALE HIRSCHMAN

before you get tired of the "sweet" taste. And when that happened, Jeff and Jimmy learned how a little bit of compromise can go a long way. They decided to have "just one" beer and then just "one more" beer, which led to "one more," and so on and so on, until ...

Speculation ended with their rodeo team coach receiving a phone call in the wee hours of the morning. As their coach answered the aggravating, inconvenient phone call, the voice on the other end identified himself as a member of the local police department and he had two of the coach's team members in custody for DUI.

"Any of my men's team members but those two," was the coach's reply to the officer as he gave the names of the two incarcerated team members. Identification was confirmed, and the coach headed to the drunk tank.

Apparently, as Jeff and Jimmy were heading back to our room, they discovered that an inconsiderate imbecile planted a light pole right in the middle of the road, or at least what they thought was the road. Even though their rate of speed was not much, it's amazing how much damage can be inflicted upon a moving vehicle when the brakes are not taken advantage of. The two-month-old car was totaled; however, pilot and co-pilot escaped without any serious boo-boos.

No one in this world is perfect except Jesus, but provin' it by several public examples can take a real toll on a person's ego. Or as my pastor says, "You don't have much problem with pride when you're getting your rear kicked." Jeff and Jimmy were not having a problem with pride at this time in their lives. Because of their stance for Jesus Christ, it brought a lot more scrutiny on their display of human weaknesses. Plus the fact that they were hosting the leader of their cowboy church services and Bible study in their motel room: me.

Neither one of them came directly back to the motel room upon their release from the calaboose, but Jimmy sent word to me that he wanted to talk to me. Jimmy and I had been close friends for quite a while. I helped him get started in rodeoing; and in fact, we hit the road and rodeoed together throughout the summer months. I also had the privilege of being a part of him growing in his walk with Jesus.

DALE HIRSCHMAN

As I drove to the designated meeting area, I rehearsed in my mind what I was going to say to him. I have to admit that since I was his spiritual big brother, I was going to chew his tail out and let him know how much he had screwed up with his compromise. I had my self-righteous six-shooters slung on my hips; and they were loaded for bear, as I was fixin' to tell him just what he was needin' to do now to make amends for his mistakes.

I was primed and ready as I turned the corner to head up the street to the meeting place. I was God's representative headed on a mission. Then I felt the presence of God fill my pickup. Now, some might think I'm getting a little weird here; but let me tell you that I could feel almost a tangible presence of God in the pickup, to the point that my driving slowed way down. Then I heard the voice of God—not an audible voice, but a voice spoke loud and clear to my spirit. This was not the "still small voice" that Elijah experienced. And I know that God will speak to us in a kind, loving, compassionate, Fatherly way. However, this time it was Almighty God talking to me!

You tell him—Man, I was listening close—*You tell him he's still my child,* rang loud and clear through my mind. Any self-righteousness was ripped out of me, and I felt unbelievably humble at that moment. There was no way I could do anything but be obedient to the voice of God, and I knew I had better be extremely careful in my attitude and the words that I was to speak. I was dealing with a child of the Most High God who was hurt, and he did not need a self-righteous jerk running his mouth.

As I pulled up and got out of the pickup to talk to Jimmy, we exchanged greetings; and then I told him, "Jimmy, God told me to tell you something."

Jimmy's head dropped, and he gazed off. You could almost see the guilt weighing him down, as he was ready for the oncoming rebuke.

"Jimmy," I said, "God told me to tell you that you're still His child."

Jimmy's eyes glossed over; and you could almost see the guilt being ripped off his shoulders as his whole posture changed from the whipped, defeated person to one who was accepted by his heavenly Father. I really couldn't tell much about his expression after that because my eyes were filled with a liquid form and things were quite blurry for the next couple of minutes. We talked about the next steps we needed to do, and we had a good visit while we were both experiencing the forgiveness of God. Truthfully, I believe that God was probably more disappointed with me and my self-righteous attitude than with Jimmy making the mistakes that he did.

We all went back to the motel room and hung out for a while. I tried to talk to Jeff a little but, he wasn't feelin' too good and really wasn't in the mood to talk. Trust me. My attitude was a lot better when I started to talk to Jeff than what it was when I started to talk to Jimmy.

While we were in the motel room that afternoon, I heard the voice of God again.

"Okay. You're through here. You can go home now," God said.

I packed my bags, said my good-byes, and left. I didn't hang around for the rodeo performance that night or try to talk the Holy Spirit into letting me stay longer. I knew better. I just headed south. I was missing my family anyway.

DALE HIRSCHMAN

As I was making the drive home, I started reflecting on what I had just been a part of, how God, in His awesome wisdom, started working in my family three months earlier so that I would be where He wanted me when He wanted me there. I thought how He had me drive twenty hours one way just to tell one of His kids who had made a mistake that he was still His child; how God had me be the one there to say it because it would be received better from me than probably anyone else; and then for me to leave Bozeman as soon as I was through and drive the twenty hours home.

As I was reflecting, I thought about how the angel in the sixteenth chapter of Mark, verses 6–7 (NKJV) told the ladies at Jesus' tomb:

> "Do not be alarmed, you seek Jesus of Nazareth, who was crucified. He is risen! He is not here. See the place where they laid Him. But go tell His disciples and Peter that He is going before you…"

Peter had just gotten through denying Jesus and then watching Jesus die on the cross. Knowing that he had failed so miserably and then watching Jesus die with no apparent hope of reconciliation between the two of them had to have Peter feeling crushed. The guilt was probably about to cave him in, and then God made the effort to individually let him know that he was still on the team. His life still mattered.

If you at one time had a relationship with Jesus and you've made some drastic choices where you have failed miserably or maybe you just drifted away from Christ 'till there seems to be such a great distance between you and Jesus, God wants me to tell you something.

"You're still His child."

Return to Jesus and receive forgiveness and freedom from guilt. Your life still matters.

Don't make me drive twenty hours just to tell you!"

DALE HIRSCHMAN

e|LIVE

listen|imagine|view|experience

AUDIO BOOK DOWNLOAD INCLUDED WITH THIS BOOK!

In your hands you hold a complete digital entertainment package. In addition to the paper version, you receive a free download of the audio version of this book. Simply use the code listed below when visiting our website. Once downloaded to your computer, you can listen to the book through your computer's speakers, burn it to an audio CD or save the file to your portable music device (such as Apple's popular iPod) and listen on the go!

How to get your free audio book digital download:

1. Visit www.tatepublishing.com and click on the e|LIVE logo on the home page.
2. Enter the following coupon code:
   ab47-c213-1064-e020-86eb-0688-3308-76e7
3. Download the audio book from your e|LIVE digital locker and begin enjoying your new digital entertainment package today!